R🌸SE of Sharon

New Quilts from an Old Favorite

American Quilter's Society

P. O. Box 3290 • Paducah, KY 42002-3290

www.AmericanQuilter.com

Sponsors

Thanks to the following sponsors:

Quality Polyester Products for Home and Industry

JANOME
Because You Simply Love To Sew™

Editor: Linda Baxter Lasco
Graphic Design: Lynda Smith
Cover Design: Michael Buckingham
Quilt Photography: Charles R. Lynch
(unless otherwise noted)

Library of Congress Cataloging-in-Publication Data

　　Rose of Sharon: new quilts from an old favorite / by American Quilter's Society.
　　　　p.　　　cm.
　　Summary: "Winners and finalists from the New Quilts from an Old Favorite contest at the Museum of the American Quilter's Society. Quilters demonstrate their interpretations of the classic block Rose of Sharon. Designs feature a variety of construction methods, embellishment ideas, and creative fabric selections."-- Provided by publisher.
　　ISBN 978-1-57432-924-7
　　1. Quilting 2. Quilting--Patterns. I. American Quilter's Society
TT835.R6715 2007
746.46'041--dc22

　　　　2007004727

Located in Paducah, Kentucky, the American Quilter's Society (AQS) is dedicated to promoting the accomplishments of today's quilters. Through its publications and events, AQS strives to honor today's quiltmakers and their work and to inspire future creativity and innovation in quiltmaking.

Additional copies of this book may be ordered from the American Quilter's Society, PO Box 3290, Paducah, KY 42002-3290; 800-626-5420 (orders only please); or online at www.AmericanQuilter.com. For all other inquiries, call 270-898-7903.

Proudly printed and bound in the
United States of America

Dedication

The Museum of the American Quilter's Society has created this contest to recognize and share with others the fascinating variety of interpretations that quilters bring forth from a single traditional quilt pattern. This book is dedicated to all those who see a traditional quilt block and can visualize both its link to the past and its bridge to the future.

The Museum of the American Quilter's Society (MAQS)

"Honoring Today's Quilter"

QUILT MUSEUM

MAQS is an exciting place where the public can learn more about quilts, quiltmaking, and quiltmakers, and experience quilts that inspire and delight.

MAQS seeks to celebrate today's quilts and quiltmakers through exhibits of quilts from the MAQS permanent collection and selected temporary exhibits. By providing a variety of workshops and other programs, MAQS helps to encourage, inspire, and enhance the development of today's quilter.

Whether presenting new or antique quilts, MAQS promotes understanding of and respect for all quilts—new and antique, traditional and innovative, machine made and handmade, utility and art.

Contents

While preservation of the past is a museum's primary function, its greatest service is performed as it links the past to the present and to the future. With that intention, the Museum of the American Quilter's Society (MAQS) sponsors an annual contest and exhibit called New Quilts from an Old Favorite.

Created to acknowledge our quiltmaking heritage and to recognize innovation, creativity, and excellence, the contest challenges today's quiltmakers to interpret a single traditional quilt block in a work of their own design. Each year contestants respond with a myriad of stunning interpretations.

Rose of Sharon: New Quilts from an Old Favorite is a wonderful representation of these interpreta-tions. You'll find a brief description of the 2007 contest, followed by a presentation of the five award winners and the 12 finalists and their quilts.

Full-color photographs of the quilts accompany each quiltmaker's comments—comments that provide insight into their widely diverse creative processes. Full-size patterns for the traditional Rose of Sharon block are included to form the basis for your own rendition. Tips, techniques, and patterns contributed by the contestants offer an artistic framework for your own work.

Our wish is that *Rose of Sharon: New Quilts from an Old Favorite* will further our quiltmaking heritage as new quilts based on the Rose of Sharon block are inspired by the outstanding quilts, patterns, and instructions in this book.

The Contest

Although the contest encouraged unconventional creativity, there were some basic requirements for entries:

- Quilts entered in the contest were to be recognizable in some way as being related to the Rose of Sharon block.
- The finished size of the quilt was to be a minimum of 50" in width and height but could not exceed 80" in any one dimension.
- Quilting was required on each quilt entered in the contest.
- A quilt could be entered only by the person(s) who made it.
- Each entry must have been completed after December 31, 2003.

To enter the contest, each quiltmaker was asked to submit an entry form and two slides of their quilt—one of the full quilt, and a second of a detail from the piece. This was the first contest featuring an appliqué block, and quiltmakers from around the world responded to the challenge.

Three jurors viewed dozens of slides, deliberating over design, use of materials, interpretation of the theme, and technical excellence. Eventually they narrowed the field of entries to 17 finalists who were invited to submit their quilts for judging.

With the finalists' quilts assembled, three judges meticulously examined the pieces, evaluating them again for design, innovation, theme, and workmanship. First- through fifth-place award winners were selected and notified.

Each year the New Quilts from an Old Favorite contest winners and finalists are featured in an exhibit that opens at the Museum of the American Quilter's Society in Paducah, Kentucky. Over a two-year period, the exhibit travels to a number of museums across North America and is viewed by thousands of quilt enthusiasts. Corporate sponsorship of the contest helps to underwrite costs, enabling even smaller museums across the country to host the exhibit.

Annually, the contest winners and finalists are included in a beautiful book published by the American Quilter's Society. *Rose of Sharon: New Quilts from an Old Favorite* is the fourteenth in the contest, exhibit, and publication series. It joins the following other traditional block designs used as contest themes: Dresden Plate, Seven Sisters, Monkey Wrench, Feathered Star, Tumbling Blocks, Bear's Paw, Storm at Sea, Kaleidoscope, Pineapple, Mariner's Compass, Ohio Star, Log Cabin, and Double Wedding Ring.

For information about entering the current year's contest, Sawtooth: New Quilts from an Old Favorite, write to Museum of the American Quilter's Society at PO Box 1540, Paducah, KY, 42002-1540; call (270) 442-8856; or visit MAQS online at www.quiltmuseum.org.

Rose of Sharon Block

During the 1840s, floral appliqué quilts were in fashion. These quilts were most frequently rendered in red and green appliqué on a white ground and were typically fashioned in a four-block style. The red in these quilts was a colorfast dye called Turkey red, quite popular in that time of unstable dyes. Such a fabric would have been more expensive than the white ground fabric, as noted in Barbara Brackman's digital newsletter *The Quilt Detective: Clues in Style 2006*. Brackman then wonders, "Imagine how quilts might have looked were the red cheaper than the white."

A number of these red and green floral appliqué quilts now appear to be red and tan on white since the green dyes available then were fugitive, that is, they were not colorfast. The floral appliqué designs may have grown out of the folk traditions of the Germans who settled in Pennsylvania (the Pennsylvania Dutch). These Germans did not have a quilting tradition of their own and adopted the craft from their English neighbors, but used the motifs of their own heritage in their designs.

Many different flowers were depicted in this red and green style: roses, poppies, marigolds, lavender, carnations (pinks), and cockscombs to name a few. In Barbara Brackman's *Encyclopedia of Appliqué*, 28 different designs are named Rose of Sharon and one is named Rose of Sharon Cluster. Most of these designs date from the first American quilt revival of the twentieth century during the Great Depression. Only a handful date from 1880 or before. This is not so surprising since few quilt patterns were published before the Civil War.

Due to technological advances in linotype, the number of periodicals boomed after the Civil War, resulting in quilt patterns being published and syndicated, available to practically every quilter in America. Since assigning names to quilt blocks is a very late nineteenth- and early twentieth-century convention, we don't really know what the quiltmaker of the 1840s would have called her block. She may have been influenced by the Bible: "I am the rose of Sharon, and the lily of the valleys" (Song of Solomon 2:1). Pattern 11.25 in the *Encyclopedia of Appliqué* lists Ohio Rose, Rose of Sharon, and Yellow Rose of Texas as names for the same pattern.

Pieced quilt patterns must conform to a set geometry, whereas appliqué patterns do not. Therefore, one would think that appliqué block designs would be vastly different from one another. Brackman did not find this to be true. Instead she tells us that "the many duplicates [of a single pattern] indicate that patterns were passed around in some fashion." Yet each quiltmaker might change the number of buds or leaves on a particular pattern, or curve the stems. Appliqué patterns known by the traditional name of Rose of Sharon are closely related to the Whig Rose, Ohio Rose, English Rose, California Rose, Democratic Rose, Tea Rose, and Spice Pink patterns, all found in quilts dating to the 1840s.

Whatever the exact design, whatever the name, and whatever the influence, the Rose of Sharon is a classic appliqué design. The Rose of Sharon quilts of one hundred and sixty years ago are a warm, tangible reminder of our needlework past and the women who stitched them. The innovative Rose of Sharon interpretations of the present honor those quilters of the past with their energy and verve.

Judy Schwender
Curator of Collections and Registrar
Museum of the American Quilter's Society

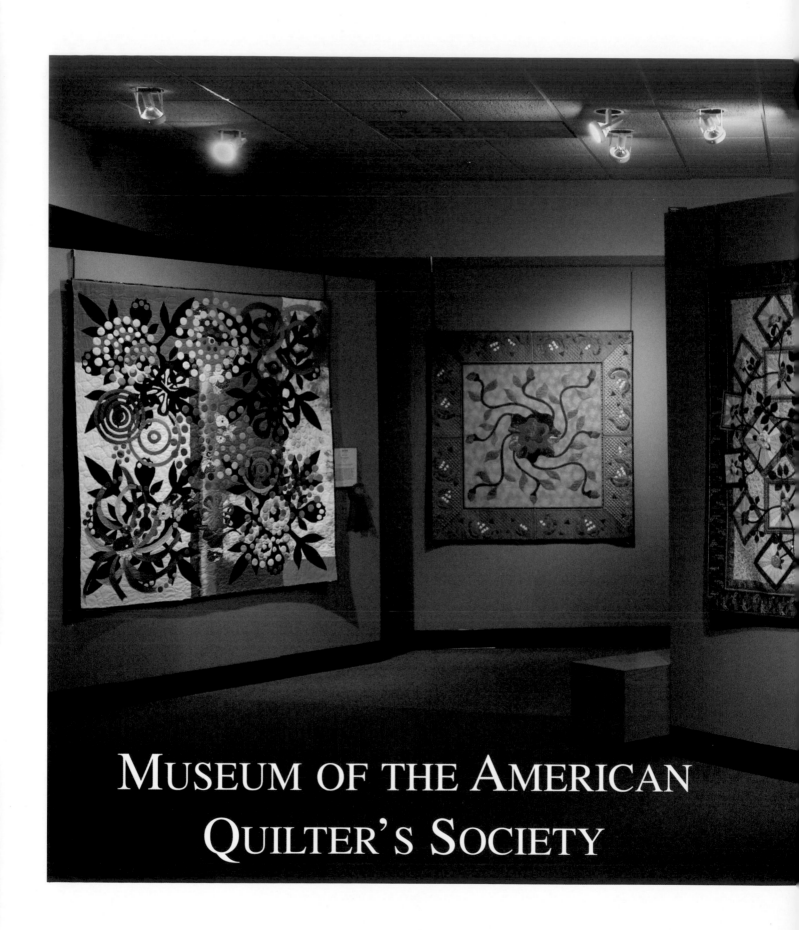

MUSEUM OF THE AMERICAN QUILTER'S SOCIETY

215 Jefferson Street • Paducah, Kentucky 42001 • www.quiltmuseum.org • (270) 442-8856

Helen's photo by Lisa Brown for Yuen Lui Studio

First Place

Helen Remick
Seattle, Washington

I am in the midst of major life changes. A year ago I retired from an administrative position at the University of Washington and my first grandchild, Charlotte, was born at about the same time. I enjoyed the intellectual challenges of my work and used quilting as a way of relaxing. Retirement has allowed me to explore more fully my creative interests and abilities.

My sense of time and how to use it is undergoing intriguing changes that give me the freedom to create. My husband, Jack, is a writer and our house hums with creative activity. My time is limited only by frequent cross country trips to visit Charlotte, our daughter Elizabeth, and her husband Yuki.

I like exploring. Within my explorations are themes that span long periods of time. M.C. Escher and op artist Bridget Riley have intrigued me for years and inform my sense of design. I love Islamic art. I first incorporated an Islamic pattern into a needlepoint project over 40 years ago. I never know quite how these interests and themes will appear in any given quilt, but appear they do.

Inspiration and Design
For this design challenge I chose to explore pentagonal symmetry to reflect the Rose of Sharon as it appears in nature. The quilt combines pentagons with spirals. My interest in both of these elements stems from a trip to Paris several years ago. I took as many pictures of spiral staircases (the Arc d'Triomphe has an especially wonderful one) as of all the other sights. I found

SPINNING OUT SPINNING IN 4
74" x 70½"

I now have a better understanding of why quilt patterns are usually not based on the pentagon. Bias edges abound.

Fig. 1. Generated spiral design

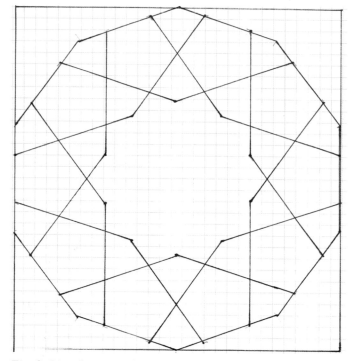

Fig. 2. Line drawing of overall design

Fig. 3. Paper-piecing section

several wonderful books on Islamic design at the Institut du Monde Arabe.

The overall design is derived from an Islamic pattern of overlapping pentagrams, as described by Keith Critchlow in *Islamic Patterns, an Analytical and Cosmological Approach*. The leafy spirals owe their beginnings to the Natural Intelligence Custom Fibonacci Spiral Generator, a computer program written by Ned May, a Virginia artist. Fibonacci was an Italian mathematician who explored a mathematical series in which each new number is the sum of the previous two.

With the generator, the user puts in a design or photograph and the program returns a spiral design. I put in triangles and generated the spirals used in several sizes on the quilt top (fig. 1). The spirals draw the viewer into and out of the quilt, depending on which color the viewer follows.

I now have a better understanding of why quilt patterns are usually not based on the pentagon. Bias edges abound. Drafting tools do not come with 72-degree angles. The shapes do not fit readily into rectangular quilts. However, the resulting design is interesting in part because the angles and relationships are unexpected.

Techniques

I like the process of drafting designs. No doubt I would be better at it had girls been allowed to take drafting when I was in high school. I draft my designs full size to ensure that each piece will fit with its neighbors.

Overall Design

I determined the final size of the quilt, keeping in mind the dimension requirements of the competition. I added elements to a sketch from *Islamic Patterns* and fit the design into a rectangular shape. I made a line drawing of the overall design (fig. 2). The spirals and flowers had to fit within the spaces created by this design.

Spirals

I used elements of the generated spiral design and enlarged them to fit the center space of the overall design. I made two copies, one as a master pattern and one to cut up for paper piecing (fig. 3).

I marked the paper-piecing pattern to indicate how each section fits with the one next to it and numbered them for final piecing. I fussy-cut the green fabric so that the green was darker as the triangles approached the center of the design. The smaller spirals used a variety of green fabrics. The finished spirals were appliquéd onto black fabric.

Flowers

The flowers were created by following lines of the spiral design (fig. 4). The center of the flower was drawn freehand and in most sizes is green, as is the center of the actual flower. The petals were appliquéd onto the center, and the finished flowers appliquéd onto the spirals or the background fabric. The flowers were fussy-cut.

Corners

A ten-sided figure does not fit neatly into a rectangle. The two "legs" at the corners are of different shapes. I drew a large flower, again using the spiral form, and made triangular leaves from the same fabric as the central spiral. I placed them where they seemed most pleasing, using half as many leaves on one leg as on the other (fig. 5). The flowers and leaves were appliquéd to the black background.

Assembly and Finishing

The assembly was challenging. I rough-cut the various background pieces for each spiral and stay-stitched the edges at the approximate finished size. Appliquéd pieces were laid out on the master pattern. I laid the checkered fabric over the pieces, and assembled the top a bit at a time. Perle cotton was hand-couched along the edges of the checkered fabric.

I wrote an essay about the quilt and the mathematics behind it and used it for the quilting design. Only words and parts of words should be discernible. I did not intend for the viewer to stand in front of the quilt reading. The writing was intended to add a layer of mystery to the quilt.

Fig. 4. Outline of flower shape

Fig. 5. Corner detail

Second Place
Mary Ann Herndon
The Woodlands, Texas

My introduction to quiltmaking came over twenty-five years ago when I first I attended a meeting of the Houston Quilt Guild. Yvonne Porcella was the speaker—need I say more. From that night on, I was hooked. I started off with traditional patterns and lessons, but grew to be more interested in developing and planning original pieces. Along the way, there have been many quilters who have influenced my work. I also find inspiration from artists in other mediums such as painting, decorative design, book illustrations, and fused glass art.

Before my retirement, I was a teacher and a school system library director. From that experience, I discovered that children's book illustrations were some of the best art around. That, too, has played a part in my development as a quilt designer.

Since my three children are all grown, I have all the time and space that I want (almost!) to devote to quilting. To top this off, my husband encourages me in this pursuit. It's an ideal situation. There is one fly in the ointment. Lately there's been competition for my quilting time, thanks to my introduction to fused glass art by my daughter-in-law, Robin. This is somewhat eased by the fact that the kiln is at her home, three hours away.

Inspiration and Design
When planning this quilt, I hand-dyed fabrics for the background that would complement the black silhouettes of the Rose of Sharon and at the same

RIO ROSIE

77½" x 77½"

I discovered that children's book illustrations are some of the best art around; they have played a part in my development as a quilt designer.

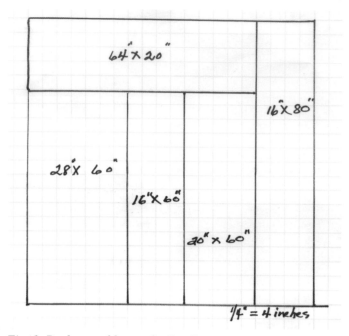

Fig. 1. Background layout for RIO ROSIE

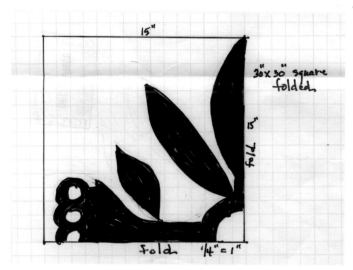

Fig. 2. Quarter template for Rose of Sharon

time highlight the collage elements. I knew I wanted oranges, pinks, and reds. Choosing colors for the appliqué elements that contrast with the background allows the viewer to appreciate the design of the overlays.

Circles were a major design element that I found easy to construct using the method described in Quilt Construction. Using gradated fabric for the circles added to the interest of the collages. I felt the design needed more direction, so I used a black-and-white commercial print and collaged diagonally across the quilt. I rejected a border.

Quilting various size circles in the black areas seemed to be an appropriate foil for the busy surface design. Black thread was used to quilt around the four Rose of Sharon appliqués and all the collage designs, while multicolor threads were used to quilt the circles in the background.

This would be an easy and fun quilt to make your own by simply varying the background and choice of collage colors and elements.

Quilt Construction

1. Choose your colors for the background. It's probably easiest to start with gradations of one color. Put your choices on your design board. If you like them, they'll be great.

2. Determine the size of your quilt and cut blocks of color for the background or substitute a wholecloth piece you love (fig. 1).

3. For the appliquéd Rose of Sharon blocks, cut four 30" black squares. Fold each in fourths, draw the quarter Rose of Sharon shape on the folded fabric, and cut out on the drawn line (fig. 2). Arrange these on the background and appliqué by the method you like best. Cut out the design ³⁄₁₆" beyond the drawn line if you wish to turn under the edges.

4. The fun begins when choosing and placing the collage elements. Choose contrasting colors so the elements show on the background.

5. Cut a variety of circle templates 1" to 4" in diameter from non-melting template plastic. Trace around the templates and cut out fabric circles with an additional ³⁄₁₆" to ¼" seam allowance.

6. Make a running stitch around the seam allowance. Place a template in the center of the wrong side of the circle and pull up the thread tight. Tie the thread to hold the gathers, dab the seam allowance with sizing, press until dry, and pop out the template. Appliqué to the background.

Gradations of sizes and colors make for a more interesting composition (fig. 3).

7. Most of the other elements can be made by folding a square into fourths, sixths, or eighths and cutting a shape as you would for a snowflake. Turn under the seam allowances and appliqué to the quilt.

8. After layering the back, batting, and top, quilt in black thread around all the collage elements and the four large Rose of Sharon motifs.

9. Quilt circles to fill in all the blank spaces. I used contrasting threads so that they would show and add to the design.

10. Bind the quilt in a fun fabric that complements the piece.

Fig. 3. Circles of gradated fabrics

Sherri's & Mary's photos by Diane Graham

Third Place
Sherri Bain Driver & Mary Vaneecke

Tucson, Arizona

Meet Sherri

Mom taught me to sew when I was about eight years old and I made most of my clothes for many years. Being frugal, I saved scraps thinking that I'd use them some day. In 1972 I made my first quilt —a Nine-Patch pieced with ⅝" seam allowances that I carefully pressed open. I backed that quilt with a percale sheet and used two layers of thick polyester batting because one layer just didn't seem fluffy enough. I tied it with embroidery floss, using pliers to pull the needle through those thick layers.

I made a few more equally sophisticated quilts in the following years, including a wedding quilt of 12" pinwheels cut from lemon yellow and kelly green calicoes. Fortunately I eventually met some "real" quilters and began learning how to make more attractive quilts.

My fabric stash, which used to fit in a shoe organizer, now fills one bedroom of our four-bedroom home. Another bedroom houses my sewing machine, design wall, cutting table, and all the other equipment I've accumulated for this "thrifty" hobby. My hobby has developed into a career. My quilting activities include designing, teaching, judging, writing and editing, as well as making quilts for competition and for pleasure.

I have loved every aspect of this quilting journey and I've made many wonderful friends along the way.

FLORABUNDA
55" x 55"

My quilts are all about using my favorite fabrics—usually ikats—while experimenting with shape, pattern, and color.

The annual MAQS challenge, New Quilts from an Old Favorite, has become a treat for me. I look forward each year to making a quilt especially for this contest, seeing what I can do with the featured block. Through the years, the contest has challenged me to work with some blocks that I don't particularly like, yet I have managed to transform them into quilts that reflect my style. If it had not been for this contest, I would never have considered making a Rose of Sharon quilt.

Inspiration and Design

I think of myself a piecer, not an appliquéer, so my first thought about the Rose of Sharon block was, "Can I adapt this design for piecing?" That idea led me to enlarging the center flower to reduce the background space between it and the smaller satellite flowers (fig. 1).

During this initial experimentation with altering the block, I considered which features of the design are

Fig. 1. Initial sketch for center motif

Fig. 2. Pieced leaf

crucial and which could be eliminated without losing the essence of the traditional Rose of Sharon. I decided that the basics of this block were one large flower in the center surrounded by eight smaller flowers with stems connecting them to the center blossom.

My first sketches did not include leaves, but I eventually decided that they were an important feature. I didn't want to break up the background shapes between the large and small flowers by adding leaves, so I pruned away a bit of each large petal to make leaves.

I chose a green ikat stripe about the same value as the petal fabric so the petal shape would remain intact. I divided each leaf to create a thin slice for a darker, narrower shape with stripes going in a different direction to add dimension to the leaf. The green color and stripes suggest leaves with veins (fig. 2).

I drafted the full-size pattern on freezer paper using a yardstick compass for the large circle. For the curves of the large and small petals, I used a seamstress curve, or fashion ruler, left over from my long-ago garment-making days.

Although my initial thought was to piece this whole quilt, I ended up doing quite a bit of appliqué after all. I pieced the smaller flowers into a semicircle shape and appliquéd them to a piece of background fabric. I edged each semicircle with a bias strip to make it easy to machine zigzag the center appliqué to the pieced background.

FLORABUNDA was made in two main sections. The flower portion was pieced and appliquéd and the simple geometric background was pieced. I designed the background on graph paper and was pleased with its proportions. The final details were fussy-cutting stripes to make interesting centers for the flowers and making bias stems. I zigzagged these in place. To hide the stem ends, I opened a bit of the seam in the smaller center flower, tucked in the stem end, and then blindstitched the opening shut.

I was thrilled when Mary agreed to quilt this piece. As a longarm quilter, her approach to quilting is very different from mine. I knew she would create unique quilting, adding another layer of design to complement my quilt top.

Choosing Fabrics

A rough sketch and a stack of fabric are all I need to start a quilt. My first fabric choice for FLORABUNDA was an ikat with subtle variations of reds and oranges. Then I added other ikats and stripes that included red, but also brought in a few other colors. I like each color decision to be supported by the colors appearing several places in a quilt, usually in different variations. This approach to building a color palette helps unify a quilt.

Color is a subject that can be studied for a lifetime without revealing all of its mysteries. Here are a few observations I have made:

- Nothing exists without its opposite. In quilting terms, that means nothing is seen without contrast. This includes contrast of value (light versus dark), temperature (warm versus cool colors), and saturation or purity (clear versus muted).

- Viewers' eyes will be drawn to the areas of highest value contrast, so place them consciously.

- Be aware of undertones that characterize a color as warm or cool.

- Black isn't always the best choice for a dark. I think dark darks that aren't really black enhance my color choices better than a true black. A rusty red on a deep, inky purple sings where it might croak on black.

- Audition fabrics at the distance from which your quilt will be viewed.

- At a distance, colors in a quilt will mix optically. It's as if someone stirred together different color paints—if stirred slowly, part of the paint will blend while other bits of paint will keep their color identities. I look for fabrics that have this quality.

- Be willing to reject a favorite fabric if it does not enhance your quilt.

- Trust your eyes no matter what color theories you've read or heard about. Theories can be disproved and rules have exceptions.

Meet Mary

My sister, Nanci, first introduced me to quilting via a round robin Seminole quilt project. I didn't like the way my fabric choices came together and that quilt top is still in strips. I did catch the quilting bug, however, and within five years, I started my own longarm quilting business, El Sol Quilting Studio.

Sherri has an amazing sense of color and she juxtaposes curves and straight lines beautifully in FLORABUNDA. When she asked me to quilt this piece for the contest, I was thrilled. My goal for the quilting was to enhance the overall movement and composition of her design.

In keeping with the theme, I turned to Jodi Robinson's book *Creative Alternatives for Traditional Favorites* for inspiration. I have always liked Robinson's clamshell design alternatives. That same clamshell shape radiates from the center of Florabunda and from that I had my theme for the quilt design (fig. 3).

With the help of some circular grid paper I adapted one leafy clamshell alternative to radiate from the center of the quilt. A leafy background fill completed the center. I put the same clamshell design with its more traditional setting in the center border. The remaining borders have a leafy feather-type variation in keeping with the overall floral theme of the quilt.

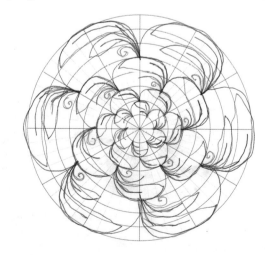

Fig. 3. Mary's initial drawing for quilting the center motif

Fourth Place

Ann Horton

Redwood Valley, California

I have been quilting for more than 25 years and show no signs of letting up. How do I fit quilting into my life? I would have to say that the challenge is more aptly stated as "How do I fit my life around my quilting?"

As a psychotherapist working intensely with the personal aspects of people's lives, and as a musician sharing the art of music making, I have many opportunities for creative work. Yet with quiltmaking, I am struck by the power of creating a piece with a tangible result—a piece of work that I can hold, visually explore, and hope that it will carry my expression to others' eyes and hearts.

Quilting is at the same time both intensely personal and a vehicle for connection with others. I find that I need the quiet, absorbed private time in my studio, and then crave the connection with the outside world of quilt shows, publications, and experiences that allow us as artists to share our work.

I take advantage of many opportunities to show my quilts and the New Quilts from an Old Favorite contest is one of my favorites. While my work continues to move towards more variations of art quilting and techniques, I feel ever inspired by the roots and traditions of quilting.

As I write this, my filmmaker son, Zach, is shooting a film near our home. My involvement on the set has been a fascinating mix of watching the art of the actors, my director son, and the professional crew work their magic. "It's just like a quilt!" I say as I see this fable unfold. Quilting is my metaphor for much of life—the delightful interweaving of experience and dreams

Ann's photo by Jessica Horton

THE ROSE PALACE
61" x 79"

I love the challenge of mixing the history and story of a particular quilt block with the expanding art quilt world of appliqué, embellishment, and design.

into the artist's finished piece that reaches out with a language of its own.

Inspiration and Design

THE ROSE PALACE began with a vendor's enticing display of vintage silk embroideries from India. A small strip of silk embroidered with peacocks and elephants caught my eye. I purchased several pieces thinking, "Someday, I'd like to make a quilt about India." As I was brainstorming ideas for the New Quilts from an Old Favorite contest, I remembered the silks and wondered if I could design my quilt to reflect the exotic beauty of an Indian garden or perhaps a palace courtyard.

In a frenzy of excitement, I began to pull fabrics from my stash looking for those with a special "Indian" feel. Next, I began to explore my collection of digitized embroidery designs. I found hundreds of fabrics and designs that I felt I could adapt to the work. The next step was to research how Indian artisans use embroidery and design.

My excitement grew as I played with a quick sketch of a Rose of Sharon block that I could tweak into a beaded, mirrored, and thread-embellished piece. Starting with these blocks and my exotic fabrics, I hand appliquéd the roses, then added machine blanket stitch and shisha mirrors (fig. 1).

I chose to align the blocks down the center of the quilt and added the clamshell side panels to showcase the many embroideries and fabrics I wished to use (fig. 2).

Fig. 1. Detail of rose embellishments

Fig. 2. Embroidered clamshells

The ivory columns seemed a natural way to separate the sections, and the stairs at the bottom would provide the background for the large appliquéd peacocks. I had a flamboyant embroidery of an exotic bird I felt I could use in the final border (fig. 3).

I designed border appliqués using elements from the Rose of Sharon blocks. The silk vintage peacock-and--elephant embroidered strip would run across the top. The round chalka embroidery would be the crowning edifice for my palace scene, but it would leave me with a curved quilt top (fig. 4, page 26). I decided to insert a sky behind the palace roof to suggest stars, while allowing for a straight hanging sleeve.

My design was complete, except for six months of sewing, embellishment, and trapunto quilting to echo the Rose of Sharon appliqués!

Techniques – Embellishments

I feel the standout feature of THE ROSE PALACE is its treasure-laden look. Certainly the appliqué, piecing, and quilting give an appropriately exotic feeling, but it is the embellishments that take the quilt beyond the expected.

The pieces I had purchased were already heavily embellished. To use them effectively, I would need to balance their opulence with added elements of my own. I feel this is the first step in appropriate use of embellishments—to maintain a balance of elements.

Since I love to use digitized embroidery on my quilts, I looked for embroideries of flora and fauna that might be associated with India. The thread colors were selected to complement the jewel-toned fabrics. Embroideries were sized and manipulated to blend and fit into the clamshells. I like my embroideries to be hidden treasures for the eye to discover. Over 100 different embroideries from the Husqvarna Viking embroidery collections were used.

The Rose of Sharon appliqués were accentuated with rayon thread blanket-stitching. The addition of the shisha mirrors echoed the mirrors in the Indian embroideries and added reflected light.

Fig. 3. Exotic bird embroidery

Beading was a major contributor to the quilt (and a major commitment on my part to hand bead it!). Beading in the Rose of Sharon block flowers was balanced with more beads in the border flowers. When I added the upper section of the quilt, the stars were beaded as well.

My initial plan was to simply quilt lines in the long ivory columns. I had added an extra layer of batting under the columns for extra dimension but the quilt would not let me be. Again and again, I fretted over those columns. Finally, I gave in and lavishly beaded them. This provided the rich color and sparkle of light I was seeking.

I designed the placement of the appliquéd peacocks' tail feathers to complement the curved steps and clamshells. An extra layer of batting helped the birds stand out from the steps. Hand-couched rayon cording filled in the edges of the appliqué. The rayon cording was variegated in color and helped to move the eye around the birds (fig. 5).

Fig. 4. Attaching round chalka embroidery

Fig. 5. Peacock feather embellishments

The embroidery on the heads of the birds was done separately on several layers of water-soluble stabilizer and sewn onto the birds with more beads. I added shisha-mirrored eyes and hand stitched feathers around the neck and head. Rayon cording was used in rich colors to make these silly courtyard birds come alive (fig. 6).

I decided to bead the long legs of the birds to secure them to the lower border's flowers, thus connecting the border elements to the courtyard and palace itself. The little beaded caterpillar was a playful touch and gave a reason for the one bird to be bending low. The final embellishment was the trapunto quilting in the outer borders, echoing the Rose of Sharon elements.

This quilt is "over the top" with embellishments but works because of the exotic theme. That word "balance" again comes to mind. In THE ROSE PALACE, I feel I have achieved a rich and treasure-filled tribute to the dreamy, faraway Indian palaces of my imagination.

How-to photos by the quiltmaker

Fig. 6. Embroidery detail

Jane's photo by Kyla A. Wells

Fifth Place

Jane Wells

Fort Wayne, Indiana

I have enjoyed sewing since I was in high school, especially stuffed animals, kids' clothes, and other crafty things. My mother passed her joy of sewing on to her four daughters. About five years ago, a good friend asked me to take a quilting class with her but I was not interested because I felt that I didn't want the mess of a box of fabric sitting around the house. Needless to say, Lynne was persuasive and I now have many drawers full of must-have fabrics.

Quilting is a gift I give myself. Never have I felt so encouraged to tap my creative side. Color makes me happy and all the interesting effects I can get by putting different colors together make me delirious! I quilt because I want to but also because I need to.

I seek out interesting quilt classes and find that the teachers (even those who are world famous) are warm and wonderful. In my teaching, I have never met a student I didn't like. I joined my church's quilt guild where I am blessed to be surrounded by smart, friendly, and encouraging women. Best of all, quilting has given me friendship and a business partnership with my sister, Linda Johnson, who is also a finalist in this contest.

My sister Linda and I are the business part of our little quilting group. My husband affectionately dubbed us "the Crafty Ol' Broads." Through this name we team teach, import and resell wonderful hand woven Guatemalan fabric, and design and sell unique quilt patterns.

I am especially inspired by things of nature including flowers, leaves, animals, and landscapes.

WHO LET THE DOGS OUT?

54½" x 79"

*It was especially rewarding to me when our friends
could pick out which pup on the quilt was theirs!*

I look for quilting designs everywhere—in building structure and design, magazine ads, and other art. Sometimes a color combination in nature or in a photo strikes me as awesome and my mind starts figuring out how to incorporate it into a quilt. I am inspired by antique quilts and intrigued by the fact that the graphic impact is much more interesting than if the points match perfectly. I appreciate good workmanship but think perfection is way overrated and often an obstacle to creativity.

I usually have a few projects going at once so that if I get bogged down or simply tired of working on one piece, I can work on something else that interests me. I think I improve an original design by giving it time to gel and mature. One of my favorite things to do is to get together with my friends while we all work on our separate quilt projects and share ideas and enthusiasm. These sessions are like an enormous group hug that lasts beyond the quilting bee.

Inspiration and Design

My family all loves animals and we share our home and acreage with many pets including llama, reindeer, goats, and, of course, a variety of dogs. WHO LET THE DOGS OUT? is a tribute to our too-cute Bichon, Bizzy. Her personality is so endearing that friends begged us to help them find a dog just like Bizzy. So we bred her and she had six adorable puppies. It was especially rewarding to me when our friends could pick out which pup on the quilt was theirs!

The inspiration for my background came from two patchwork-patterned boxes of tissues—one in blue and one in green. I liked the simplicity of one patch in so many shades of each color and used that design to represent sky and grass on a perfect May day.

I have wild gardens everywhere and the pups loved playing hide and seek and rolling in the flowers. Since all Bichons are white, I felt that the black-and-white borders appropriately represented the fencing that couldn't keep the pups in.

My favorite quilts always seem to be those with appliqué on pieced backgrounds. I think taking on a challenge such as the New Quilts from an Old

Favorite encourages me to push myself to the next level of design. This quilt was about seven months in the making and a big part of the time was figuring out dimensions as I constructed this quilt from five main pieces.

My design wall is my favorite quilting tool. I had drawn a few ideas around pups and the Rose of Sharon, but WHO LET THE DOGS OUT? was a design in progress on my design wall for several months. When I was almost done, I felt that the center panel lacked something and after a couple days thinking about it, came up with the additional sprigs of colorful circles emanating from the center rose—just the focus that the panel needed.

The flowers are all turned-edge appliqué using invisible thread and the blind hem. The butterflies are *broderie perse*. The Bichons were made using fusible webbing on an appliqué sheet and then placed amongst the flowers as completed dogs. I had previously made raw-edge appliqué of several other pets. I love the challenge and it helps me appreciate all the shadows and shades on an animal. A challenging but very fun and interesting part of my quilting business now includes taking photos of other people's pets and making them into art quilts.

Techniques – Puppies

I had photos of each pup blown up to give me a consistent size for the puppies' heads. Next, I traced important elements of the each puppy onto a master pattern (fig. 1). I chose at least seven shades of white, numbered them, and numbered each puppy part with its shade. Then I traced individual patterns from the master pattern.

I pressed double-sided fusible webbing onto the backs of the different fabrics, cut out and arranged the pieces for each puppy, and fused the entire pup on an appliqué pressing sheet. The complete dog was then fused onto the quilt top and embellished with decorative stitching. Most of the detail stitching was done as part of the quilting process.

The puppies and flowers were appliquéd to each section before sewing them together. I pinned back a few pieces that I wanted to reach into a neighboring section and appliquéd those pieces after the quilt was totally constructed.

Black-and-White Borders

I sewed 2½" muslin strips to the pieced blue center section, then added the green corner sections. A narrow strip of green was added to stabilize the bias edges of the quilt.

I made paper foundation patterns for the inner and outer black-and-white borders from tracing paper. I enjoyed using a variety of black-and-white fabrics given to me by friends. The inner border was appliquéd over the muslin strips with invisible thread and a blind hem stitch. The straight sides of the outer border were sewn to the narrow green strip and the wavy edge bound in red.

My sixteen-year-old daughter, Kyla, loves this quilt, so WHO LET THE DOGS OUT? will be given to her when it is returned to us. Of course, we all know it was never Kyla's fault that the real puppies got out.

Fig. 1. Master puppy pattern

Kathryn's photo by Anthony R. Pinder; how-to photos by the quiltmaker

Kathryn Botsford

Campbell River, British Columbia, Canada

I became interested in quilting in the summer of 1985. I bought some books, tools, and fabric but only dreamed until I finally started quilting in the fall of 2001. I have not looked back since. I took all the classes taught by a very talented local quilter, Carol Seeley. I feel fortunate to have had the opportunity to learn from her, as otherwise it might have taken me a lifetime to learn what I did in a few concentrated years. I have become totally consumed with quilting, having completed numerous projects involving traditional quilting, art quilting, wearable art, and accessories. Quilting is the creative expression for which I have longed.

In my professional life, I am in my thirtieth year of teaching public school. I enjoy teaching more each year and I feel learning to quilt has made me become a better teacher.

I like to enter shows, challenges, and contests because they motivate me to explore different areas of quilting. I have learned so much and improved technically as a result. My quilting is continually evolving and changing as I am learning and growing through exploring the endless possibilities quilting offers. I am not yet the quilter I want to be, but the journey is wonderful.

I was born in Germany to American parents and lived there until I was six years old. Following years in Michigan and Florida, I have lived on the northern end of beautiful Vancouver Island for 32 years. My husband and I are both animal lovers. Our dogs and two of our cats came from the local SPCA. We rescued our third cat, Porter, from life under a portable classroom. I have my husband's unconditional love and support in all that I do and all that I want to become. I am truly blessed.

METROPOLIS IN BLOOM

55" x 67"

*I used non-traditional construction methods to create
the effect of the Rose of Sharon blanketing the city.*

Inspiration and Design

The process of creating a quilt from one of my ideas is different for each quilt. Quilts pieced with traditional blocks are designed in detail on paper, especially when creating secondary designs. My art quilts are either roughly planned on paper or done spontaneously.

I had intended to make a quilt for last year's New Quilts from an Old Favorite contest. I gathered up all the fabric but by the time I got serious about making the quilt I knew I didn't have enough time to finish it. I was determined to complete a quilt for this year's contest, so I started to work on ideas last fall.

Inspired by Alexander Henry's Metropolis fabric, I decided I wanted roses blanketing a busy city of the post-Depression and World War II eras. Metropolis in Bloom is meant to convey the growth and prosperity brought to our cities in the 1940s. The gray times of the Depression were not forgotten, but our cities were in bloom and the future was bright.

Quilt Construction – Background

First, I pieced the background and borders using eight different fabrics. I sandwiched the background with the batting and backing and quilted it in diagonal lines with silver metallic thread.

I put the quilted background on the design wall and auditioned various gray-tone fabric strips. When I got the look I wanted, I machine stitched the strips to the quilted background, quilted it again with black-and-white variegated thread, and returned it to the design wall.

Blooms

I studied variations of the Rose of Sharon in two books: *Carrie Hall Blocks* by Bettina Havig and *Encyclopedia of Appliqué* by Barbara Brackman. I made a rough drawing of the Rose of Sharon block placements and made templates for two sizes of blooms and leaves (see placement diagram, page 37).

Each of the three-piece blooms was made separately with a variety of pink and red fabrics. I auditioned them on the quilted background to get a good balance of color before assembling five large and 20 small blooms.

1. Trace around the outer bloom template onto the right side of the fabric and cut out with a seam allowance of about ½".
2. Lay the bloom fabrics, wrong side down, onto a piece of Thermore® and stitch just inside the traced line. Trim the Thermore close to the stitching line.
3. Use a circle template to cut out the center for each bloom.
4. Baste under the edges of all three bloom pieces, trimming the seam allowances to about ¼".
5. Layer and appliqué the three bloom pieces together. Quilt the blooms with pink-toned variegated thread.
6. Position the blooms on the quilted background and pin in place.

Stems

I used different green fabrics for the large and small stems.
1. Cut 1½" strips for the large stems and 1" strips for the small stems.
2. Sew the strips, wrong sides together, with a ¼" seam allowance. Press the raw edges under to get ½" and ¼" wide stems.
3. Determine the approximate length of the large stems and cut 18.
4. Determine the approximate length of the small stems and cut 16.
5. Position and pin the stems onto the quilted background.

Leaves

The leaves were made in the same way as the blooms. I traced the templates onto a variety of green fabrics, cut them out with ½" seam allowances, stitched them to Thermore, quilted the veins, basted under the edges, trimming the seam allowances to ¼", and pressed the leaves.

I made 90 large leaves and 96 small leaves and pinned them to the stems on the quilted background.

Positioning and Stitching the Blocks

To accurately place the blooms, I positioned and pinned all pieces of the four Rose of Sharon blocks and the center bloom, measuring from the top, bottom, and sides.

I removed all the leaves and small blooms and created a yarn grid over the quilt. Then I adjusted and repinned the large blooms and stems, measuring to check their positioning and trimming the stems to the appropriate size (fig. 1).

After the yarn grid and the large blooms were removed, the stems were pinned more securely to the quilted background (fig. 2) and machine stitched to the quilt.

In the same way, the blooms and leaves were positioned, pinned, and machine stitched in place.

After all the pieces for the Rose of Sharon blocks were machine stitched to the quilted background, I was not happy with the way they looked, so I hand appliquéd them to the quilt (fig. 3). I have never used this method before but it seemed to work for this quilt

Binding, Label, and Sleeve
The last job was to bind the quilt, which was done by a standard method; then I made the label and sleeve. I hung and steamed the quilt to get it to hang straight.

Fig. 1. Yarn grid

Fig. 2. Stems pinned and quilted

Fig. 3. Roses appliquéd to quilt

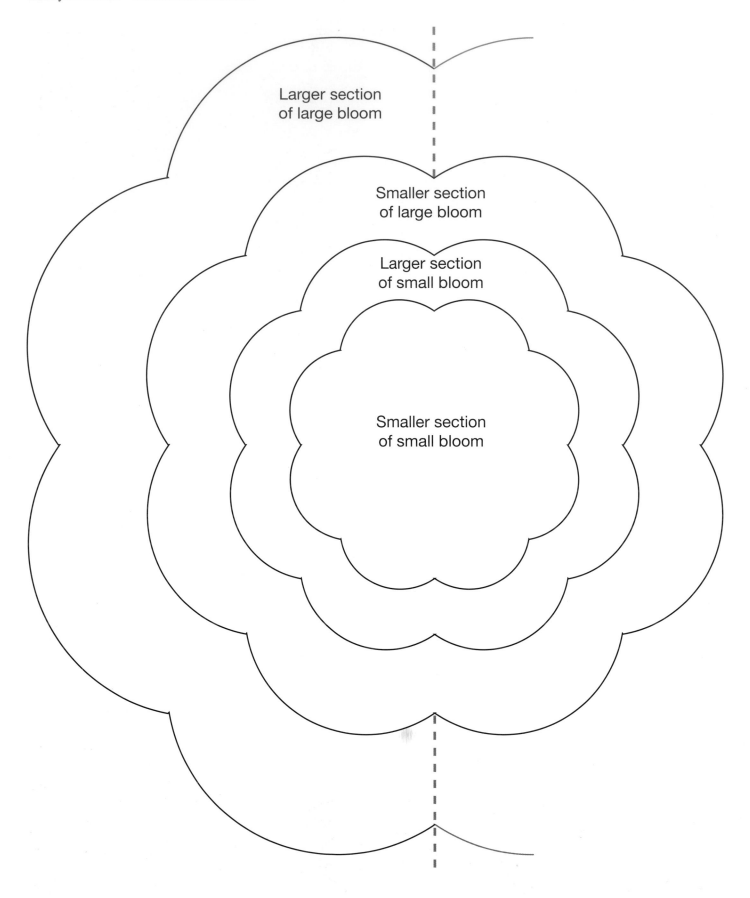

Larger section
of large bloom

Smaller section
of large bloom

Larger section
of small bloom

Smaller section
of small bloom

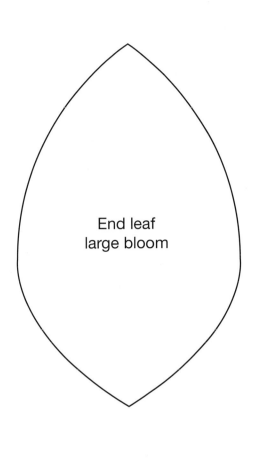

End leaf
large bloom

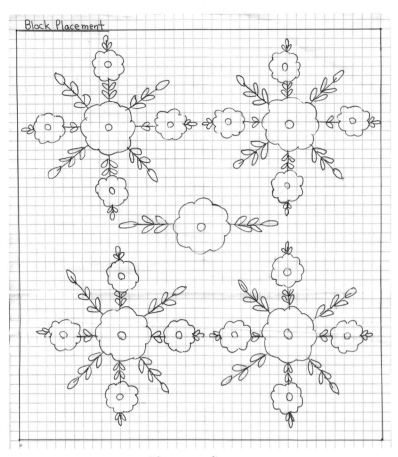

Block Placement

Placement diagram

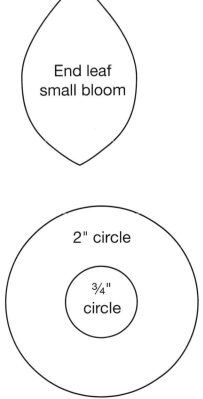

End leaf
small bloom

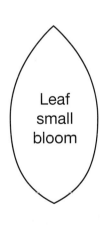

Leaf
small
bloom

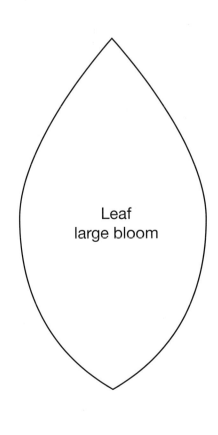

Leaf
large bloom

2" circle

¾"
circle

1¼" circle

½"
circle

Christine's photo by Portrait Corporation of America

Christine Copenhaver

Franklin, Tennessee

During the work week, I am an environmental scientist. I spend my days doing analytical things: evaluating data from hazardous waste sites, trying to figure out cleanup goals to protect human health and the environment, and writing reports (lots of reports). So, in the evenings and on weekends, it's refreshing to get out of my left-brain analytical mode and into my right-brain creative mode. There is nothing like playing with color and fabric after a long day staring at black-and-white text on a computer screen.

I learned to sew in the eighth grade. I loved it, mainly because I was on a clothing allowance and found I could have a lot more clothes if I made some of them myself. When I graduated from high school, my parents gave me a Singer Featherweight (bless them). They said it would give me something to fall back on if college didn't work out. Well, college did work out but I'm still sewing with it. In fact, it's the only sewing machine I own.

For a while between undergrad and graduate school I supported myself making slipcovers for a company that imported Scandinavian furniture. They featured hand silk-screened Marimekko® fabric from Finland that came in bold geometric designs. Oranges, yellows, reds, black-and-white, and lime greens were popular then, and I got to keep the scraps. Of course, I made some quilts. They were simple affairs with large 6"–9" blocks that showed off the fabric.

That did not exhaust my supply of Marimekko scraps and I moved several heavy boxes of them

ROSCOE ROSE
55" x 54"

When I graduated from high school, my parents gave me a Singer Feather-weight and I'm still sewing with it. In fact, it's the only sewing machine I own.

Fig. 1. Playing on the green background

Fig. 2. Adding the red fabric

around with me for 30 years—from Boston to Seattle to Utah to Southern California, back to Seattle, and finally to Tennessee, while I pursued graduate school and jobs.

In 2001, I was out of work for awhile and was somehow inspired to open up those boxes and make more quilts. After having worked almost exclusively with toned-down colors, it was quite a thrill to play with the bright, primary colors of the 1960s and '70s. Nevertheless, when I used up that fabric, I went back to my browns, rusts, and beiges and traditional blocks.

I took on the Rose of Sharon challenge to get out of my color rut and to stretch creatively. There were times when it was definitely a struggle, but I persevered and finished Roscoe Rose, which was my main goal. This was the first quilt contest I ever entered and I'm absolutely thrilled that my quilt was selected as a finalist!

Inspiration and Design

I did not have a complete vision or design for this quilt when I started but I had little vision snippets:

- A single, oversized Rose of Sharon of some sort would fill the central block.

- The background color would be something other than white.

- The central flower would be three-dimensional with probably some shade of red.

- I'd use some Dupioni silk in it somewhere.

- There would be an inner border of black and white.

- I wanted to put beads on it.

Not surprisingly, a perusal of my stash found nothing inspirational, just a half-yard of pinkish-red. I had to go fabric shopping with an open mind. First, I found the black and gold fabric that I thought would work well for bias-cut stems and the leaves. (It didn't. It was too coarse a weave for an appliqué novice.) Then, a batik lime green just jumped off the shelf and I knew I had something to work with. A remnant piece of cheddar also wanted to come with me, along with a few fat quarters of various reds for good measure.

I took it all home, slapped that green up on the design wall and started playing (fig.1). I love nineteenth-century appliqué quilts and wanted to use the traditional Rose of Sharon design of a central flower and four branches, keeping it somewhat primitive but adding something complex. It occurred to me to add a sunburst behind the central rose. I tried some impromptu rays, but had trouble with my construction technique. As always, ideas are one thing, execution is another.

So, I went out and bought Judy Mathieson's book *Mariner's Compass Quilts: New Directions.* Following her techniques, I drafted and constructed a compass using the cheddar and gold silk. After many hours, I completed the central compass, and (surprise!) it was flat. I put it up on the wall of green fabric, pinned on a pink rosette, stepped back and—it disappeared! The rays just blended into the background. All that work to no avail.

Fortunately, my friend Patty Ashworth, of the award-winning *Out-of-Towners* quilt group, was due for a visit. She suggested that I needed something behind the compass that would add contrast. I tried many colors, searched many hours in fabric stores, but didn't find anything that made me happy. Running out of time, I was forced to make a decision. I did not like the red I chose, but I made the commitment and continued on. In the end, I saw that the red makes the quilt and I am glad I used it (figs. 2–4).

The one regret I have about the quilt is that I don't know how to machine quilt. Although I love hand quilting and could do it for hours, I think the quilt could have been greatly enhanced by skillful machine quilting. Due to time constraints, I had to use fairly simple hand-quilting designs. I had many ideas for elaborate feathers and denser quilting, but my job got in the way. Someone has got to pay for a bad fabric habit!

When I get the quilt back I'm going to put beads on it.

Fig. 3. Adding the inner border

Fig. 4. Designing the outer border

Finalist

Karen G. Fisher

Tucson, Arizona

I have made art my whole life. I have degrees in sculpture and art education. Art school was a wonderful time and a great place to try working in different mediums, from wood and metal to clay, paint, photography, and fibers. In all of these mediums I enjoyed creating richly detailed and textured surfaces.

I only recently came to quilting. Like many women, I made a quilt for my first granddaughter and was immediately hooked. Even my first quilt was not traditional. I bought some beautiful hand-dyed pinks and simply started cutting and building.

Since then, I've discovered that I really enjoy the rich textures I can get when I combine multiple commercial tone-on-tone fabrics that are tightly color-coordinated, as I did with the greens in MY FATHER'S ROSE GARDEN. I often build areas of color by piecing, cutting, and repiecing fabrics to get even richer color and texture. Adding tucked areas to the fabric is another way to add texture. Tucks are becoming a signature technique for me, as I do them in almost all my quilts.

I often build my quilts in visual layers, just as I worked with layering clay and glazes when I did ceramics. Most of my designs happen in my head as I work. For some quilts, only lists of colors or numbered arrangements go on paper, so I don't have a clear idea of what the quilt will look like until it is all together.

Many of the techniques I use have evolved out of the custom dressmaking I used to do, primarily wedding dresses and costumes. My lifelong

MY FATHER'S ROSE GARDEN
67" x 67"

Tucks are becoming a signature technique for me,
as I do them in almost all my quilts.

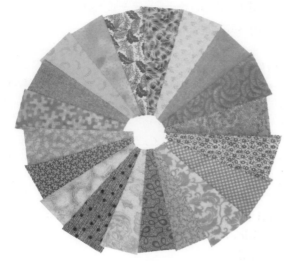

Fig. 1. Foundation-pieced Dresden Plate background

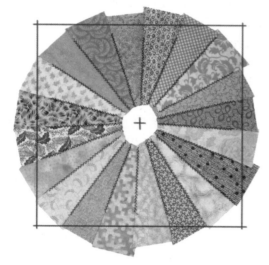

Fig. 2. Machine-embroidered seams

Fig. 3. Mitered block borders

involvement with art and design give me a wealth of resources to draw on for my own designs. One of the greatest sources of inspiration is the wonderful group of women I've met through my local quilt guild. Without their encouragement, I would not have continued to grow as an artist in this wonderful medium of quilts.

Inspiration and Design

As a nontraditional quilter, I didn't immediately see how I could use the Rose of Sharon block. Then I saw a version of the design where the smaller roses formed a secondary pattern and I was off and running.

On this quilt, I did need to make a pattern for the block sizes and background. What if I surrounded a large central block with smaller blocks and carried the rose pattern across from one to the next? I tried sizes and arrangements on graph paper to see what would work. I gathered fabrics to do the roses in *broderie perse* and made templates for the leaves. Each of the borders was simply fit in as I chose the striped fabrics to use and I figured out how to quilt it after it was all together.

I chose light green for the background. I originally planned to randomly piece the block backgrounds but decided they would be prettier in a Dresden Plate arrangement (fig.1). I finalized block sizes and used foundation piecing on fabric for construction. I machine embroidered the seams and went shopping again for striped fabrics for my borders (fig. 2). The block border stripes were mitered and blanket-stitched to the central area of each block (fig. 3).

Dressmaking methods worked for the overlapping areas and Y-seams. As the central nine blocks came together, more blanket stitching finished the edges. I looked at my initial design, which had all the blocks set at 45 and 90 degrees to each other. If I tipped the blocks slightly, the effect would be more circular. So the background shapes were altered slightly, the outer ring went on, and the outer border was appliquéd in place.

Finally it was time for the roses (fig. 4). I used bias strips for the stems, making them narrower toward the outer edges of the quilt, and fused the leaf shapes in place. Stems and leaves were all machine stitched with zigzag or blanket stitches. The roses and surrounding leaves were fused and stitched in place.

Quilting this piece was a real struggle for me. It was my largest quilt to date where I did all the work on my home machine and it was a lot of fabric to deal with! However, I had special fun with the radiating designs in the individual blocks, making the roses stand up with a pseudo-trapunto effect. I used blanket stitch for much of the quilting because it adds texture and depth to the surface. The outermost tucked border was quilted to make the tucks stand up a bit and catch the light. Beads sewn through to the back completed the quilting. Red binding and a narrow gold braid finished off the edges.

I chose to honor my father with the name of the quilt. He grew beautiful roses, which always bloomed in the spring and fall in Tucson's hot weather. My favorite of all his roses was called Sutter's Gold, a beautiful yellow climbing rose. It was the inspiration for the central rose in my quilt.

Quilt Construction

I like to use foundation piecing to build areas of color, but with a fabric backing instead of paper. The fabric stabilizes the multidirectional seams and I think it takes less time to trace the design onto the fabric squares than it takes to rip out paper later on. If I want to add embroidery to the blocks, the underlying fabric works as a stabilizer.

I found more than twenty light green fabrics for this quilt, including batiks and homespun. After precutting all my pieces, I picked the number for each block and arranged them in a circle. The foundation fabric piece was larger than the finished block size. I marked the center point and the lines for the seams. I finger-pressed each seam as it was sewn and turned under the edge of the last piece and sewed it down flat with a small zigzag stitch.

This could be done by hand, but I knew it would be covered by embroidery.

After pressing, I machine featherstitched along each seam. By doing it at this point, I could contain all my ends under subsequent layers and not have to worry about distorting the fabric later on. I didn't have to stitch to the edges because the block's border overlapped the curve. This could be hand embroidered at any stage of the construction.

I pressed the block again and used a square ruler to trim the blocks to size. The center mark helped to align the ruler.

Striped fabrics make wonderful borders and add great detail with minimum effort. The borders on the smallest blocks vary a bit because the fabrics had different width stripes. I could accommodate the variations because the borders are appliquéd, not pieced.

Lining up the stripes at the mitered corners is important, so I always pin these little seams, then press them open. The completed border is pinned flat to the block, the inner edge turned under, and blanket stitched in place. This is another place where hand embroidery will also work. By doing the embroidery at this point, I'm also working with a manageable sized piece in my machine or by hand.

Fig. 4. Broderie perse rose

Jan's photo by Eric J. Frazer

Finalist
Jan Frazer
Elwood, Victoria, Australia

I started patchwork and quilting in 1977. My husband, Eric, was doing post-doctoral research at the University of Tennessee in Knoxville. Having only just arrived from Australia, I joined nearly every class offered by the local craft shop so that I could make some friends. Fortunately, one of these classes was patchwork and quilting. My first quilt was a green-and-white Double Irish Chain, machine pieced on a borrowed machine and hand quilted. Many quilts have followed, incorporating numerous techniques and materials.

I love to experiment, and my work over the last 10 to 15 years has moved from traditional to a more contemporary art quilt style. I love the use of strong colors and utilize as many different fabrics as I can in a piece. I feel that the use of many fabrics makes the quilt more interesting. I have no formal training in color or design theory and have been reading as many books as possible on these topics.

This year I started a journal/sketch book (even though I cannot draw) so that I have a record of ideas and inspiration. I am finding this a very useful tool and wish I had done so sooner. My goal when I finished full-time work was to establish my own "style," but I find that every quilt I make is different in approach from the previous ones. Perhaps one day I will discipline myself to work on a series.

The use of a design wall is invaluable to me since I can continuously reassess the work as it progresses to ensure that the design, color, and fabric choices are in unison. As I have a mathematical background, I do not find the drafting stage of the process intimidating. This

SHARON'S REEL
50" x 50"

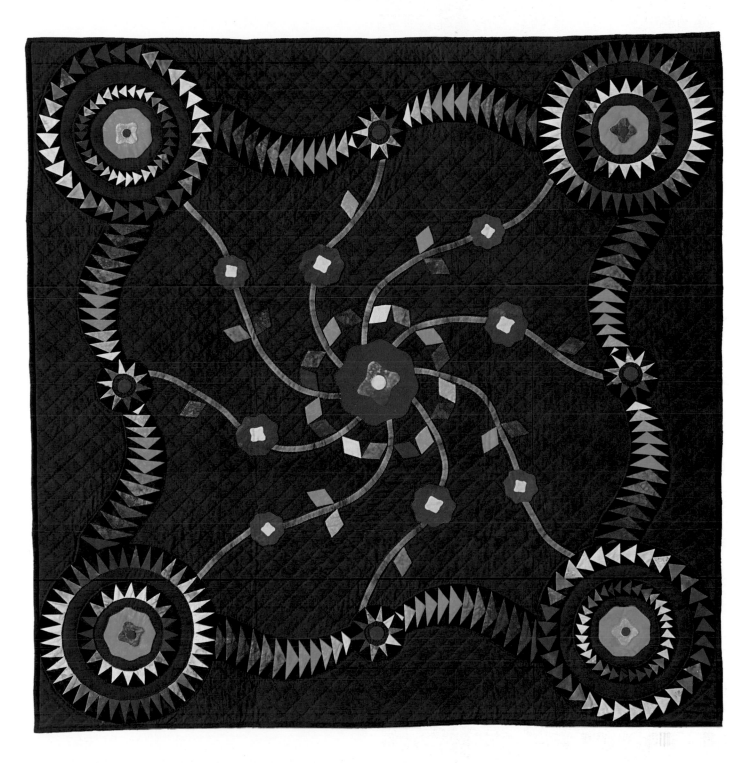

I feel that the key to a successful quilt is to allow plenty of time for the design process. Every piece in the quilt should be there for a reason.

step, like the planning stage, cannot be rushed. I recommend starting a sketch/design journal. It does not have to be a masterpiece, but can be a very useful tool.

Inspiration and Design

My source of inspiration for this quilt came from a photo of an 1840s' Pennsylvania quilt that combined a variation of the Rose of Sharon with the Sunburst pattern. The Rose of Sharon "grew" out of each quadrant of the Sunburst blocks. It was a stunning quilt!

My design process started with a 16½" Rose of Sharon block (from *Quilter's Newsletter Magazine*, July 1976). This was enlarged by 150% and placed on my design wall. A Sunburst block was drafted and also pinned up. Over the following weeks I studied these two blocks and sketched a number of rough designs (fig. 1). The ideas ranged from an overgrown wild garden with oversized flowers to the eventual basis for the final design (fig. 2). Having decided that I liked the central flower flowing out

Fig. 1. Preliminary design sketch

to the Sunburst blocks at the corners, I worked on refining this design. The remaining stems flowed to the Rose of Sharon flowers.

The use of curved Flying Geese unified the central element with the corner blocks and outer flowers. At this stage I had sketched a possible border but made no decision as to whether it would be used. The chosen design dictated a square central area so I decided to make this the minimum entry size of 50 inches. This way the option of a border was still open.

The next step was the choice of color and fabrics. I pulled possible background fabrics from my collection and found a perfect deep blue-purple piece. Unfortunately, not only was this piece too small but also I had no other fabrics to complement it. A trip to the local patchwork shop ensued and I was not leaving until I had found a background piece. A considerable time later I left with my choice, a color that was to be quite a challenge as it made many other fabrics look grey. The selection of the beautiful hand-dyed fabrics I had accumulated over the years was the perfect choice to offset this background color.

I do mainly free-motion appliqué, but felt that the design needed a more traditional approach. Appliqué with feed dogs up is a relatively new experience for me, as was the foundation piecing used for the Flying Geese and Sunburst patterns.

I love the vibrant colors of this quilt and felt that a border was not necessary. As the design of the quilt generates movement, a simple crosshatch quilting pattern was chosen, with outline quilting around the appliquéd pieces.

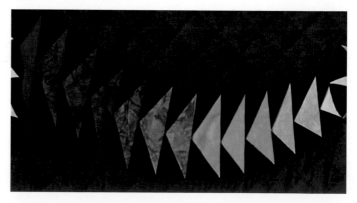

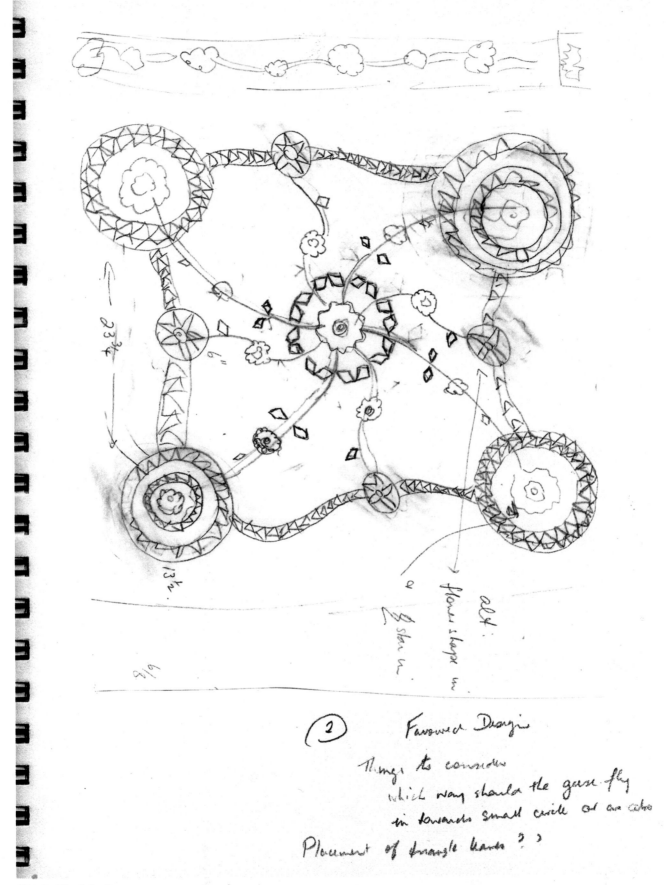

Fig. 2. Final design

Julia's photo by Amy J. Graber

Julia Graber

Brooksville, Mississippi

Sewing has been a part of my life since I learned to make my own clothes in home economics class at school. I grew up in a sewing family so my mother and sisters have been a great inspiration to me. My grandmother and aunts make quilts and have inspired some of my projects and I talk with my husband's mom and aunts about quilts. They all give me their opinions and advice on color and design. Getting together with my family each year for a week of sewing is a highlight of the year.

I so much enjoy cutting apart beautiful fabric and sewing it back together to make a quilt. Because my parents had a fabric store, I was blessed with access to a good sewing machine and have enjoyed upgrades through the years.

Paul and I have been married for 29 years and have five boys and one girl. I tied some flannel blankets for our first three children when they were babies. Now I'm trying to make them each a quilt for a wedding gift.

Inspiration and Design

The Rose of Sharon block was a real challenge for me because all the different patterns I found were appliquéd. I haven't done a lot of hand or machine appliqué so I decided to try making a very small sample quilt with one quadrant of the Rose of Sharon. I chose bright colors and fusible appliqué and it turned out to look like a frog. I call it FROG OF SHARON (fig. 1, page 52).

Next I tried using a black fabric on a bright sunset background giving the rose a silhouette look. When

PINEAPPLE ROSE & BUDS
52" x 52"

*Getting together with my family each year for
a week of sewing is a highlight of the year.*

Fig. 1. FROG OF SHARON

Fig. 2. AFRICAN ROSE

Design process photos by the quiltmaker

it was finished, it reminded me of something out of Africa, so I call it AFRICAN ROSE. (fig. 2).

Then I thought I'd try converging a Rose of Sharon quadrant (figs. 3–4).

After converging, the design was lost, so I thought I'd just put some appliqué on top and do some fancy stitches around it (fig. 5).

I still wasn't happy and left this top unfinished. Then I tried converging a complete Rose of Sharon block with rose motifs in the corners. This, too, fell by the wayside as the design was again lost (figs. 6–8).

Because I wasn't completely happy with these four quilts, I decided to abandon the appliqué technique and try something different. I had enjoyed working with the Pineapple block and making A PLATE OF PINEAPPLES for last year's MAQS contest. (It won fourth place.) I found a paper grid of Pineapple blocks in *Hall & Haywood's Foundation Quilts: Building on the Past*, by Jane Hall and Dixie Haywood and I started coloring it with colored pencils to look like a rose (fig. 9, page 54).

This had the effect that I liked without the appliqué. After sewing the blocks and top together, I decided that the four center blocks looked too square (fig. 10, pg. 54).

So I picked out the center blocks and went back to the drawing board, coloring six different variations for the center. I settled on #4 (fig. 11, page 55).

Now, I finally had a Rose of Sharon quilt top without the work of appliquéing.

The machine quilting represents a rose's stem with many thorns. The quilting caused a lot of distortion in the quilt and it needed to be blocked.

I laid a piece of heavy-duty vinyl upholstery fabric on the living room floor. I laid the quilt on top of it and squared it up, pinning it every three inches by poking pins through the quilt and vinyl and into the carpet and padding. Then I poured 1–2 gallons of water over the quilt, making sure the entire quilt got sopping wet. I soaked up the extra water around the outside with a towel. I turned a fan on and let it sit for a day or two until it was completely dry. This produced a quilt that was nice and square and that hung straight.

Fig. 5. Appliqué over convergence

Fig. 3. Before converging

Fig. 6. Center rose motif

Fig. 4. After converging

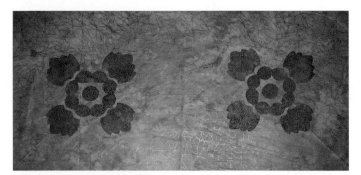

Fig. 7. Corner rose motifs

Rose of Sharon: New Quilts from an Old Favorite

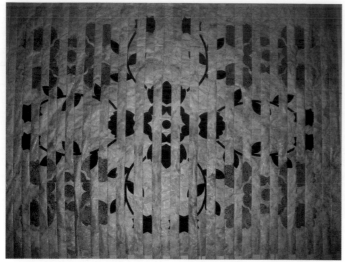

Fig. 8. After converging

Fig. 10. Too-square center

Fig. 9. Designing with the Pineapple grid

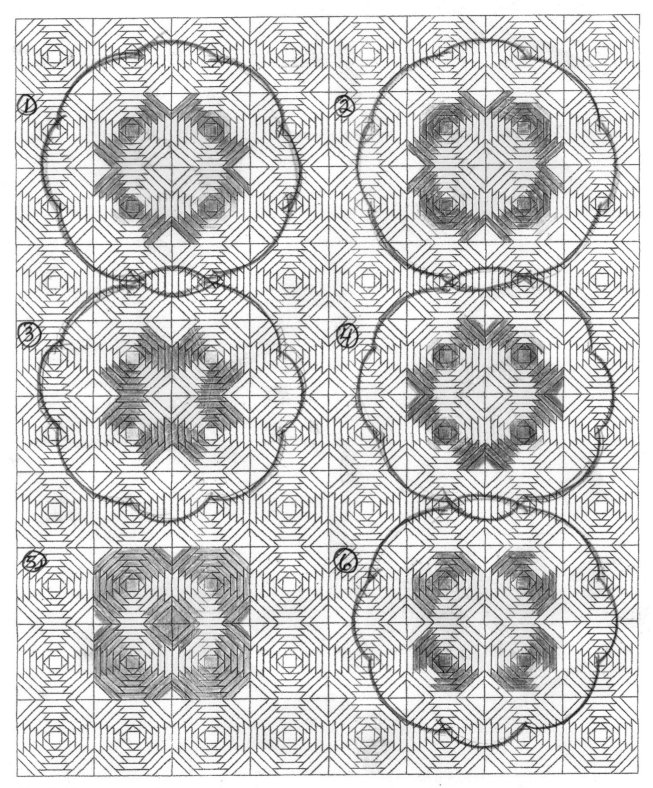

Fig. 11. Alternate center designs

Barbara Holtzman
Holyoke, Colorado

My mother taught my sisters and me to sew, and we all made clothes for quite a few years. When my kids were little I took a hand-piecing class. Instead of making a small project, I started a bed quilt. It took forever! I enjoyed the handwork but decided I liked machine stitching more.

In 2000 I came across a miniature quilting magazine and decided to make a miniature quilt. I was hooked right away. Through that project I discovered paper piecing, rotary cutting, and a whole new world. I subscribed to a quilting magazine and found out what I'd been missing. The possibilities for creativity seemed endless.

I love a challenge and especially like the New Quilts from an Old Favorite contest. I have a notebook where I write down ideas that come to me. I'm one of those people who has to think through things and plan before I can start. Most of the time, I've decided how I want to do the quilting before I even start the sewing. That may change, but it gives me a starting point.

I have found that I need to name my quilts early on. They seem more personal and are easier to create when they have a name. Naming, for me, gives the quilt a theme and a direction. If I have trouble with naming, I also seem to have trouble creating.

I love fabric—especially hand dyed and batiks. However, I must have a project in mind before I will pick up material. I'm limited on storage space so I don't have a very big stash—I share my sewing space with the computer, my husband's

Barbara's photo by Dixie Fagerlin; quilt detail photos by the quiltmaker

FIVE SISTERS
60" x 60"

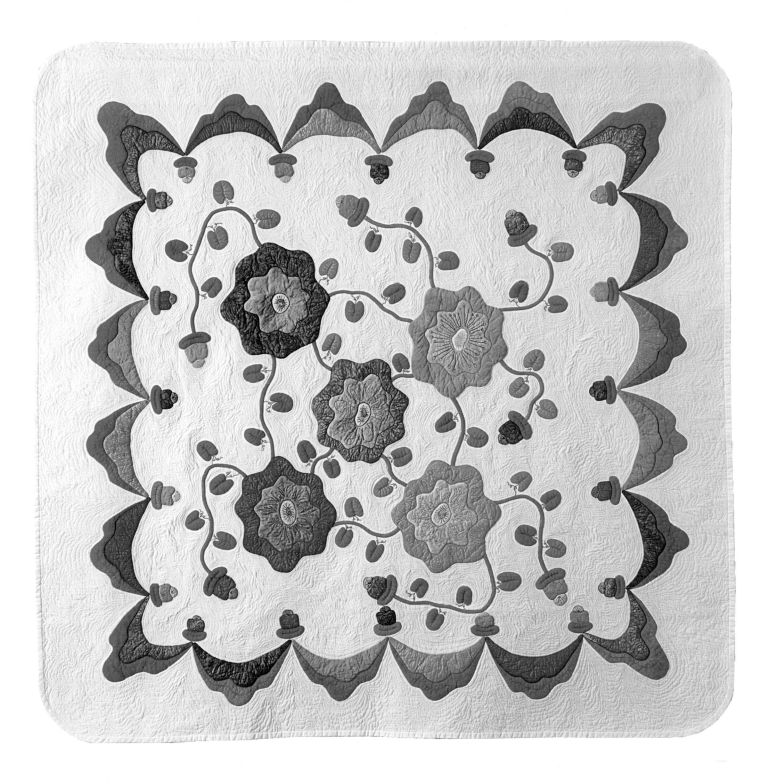

I create a schedule with each quilt—a timetable of what to get done when. I'm always adjusting the schedule, but it helps to keep me focused.

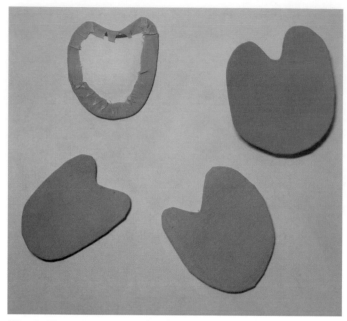

Fig. 1. Freezer-paper appliqué

fishing equipment, and the piano. The stash is in baskets in a wardrobe in our bedroom, my design wall is flannel tacked to the closet doors in my son's room (he's in college), and my basting/blocking area is the living room floor. As long as it works, I have no complaints. I just want to sew!

Inspiration and Design

I've always been close to my four sisters but since the passing of both my father and mother, they've become even more important to me. When I saw the theme Rose of Sharon and started doodling, the idea of five flowers began to grow. I'd been wanting to do a quilt that showed how we are all separate but connected. Off of each flower grows a bud—a child—or two or three, or none. Each of us is passing on our legacy in our own way.

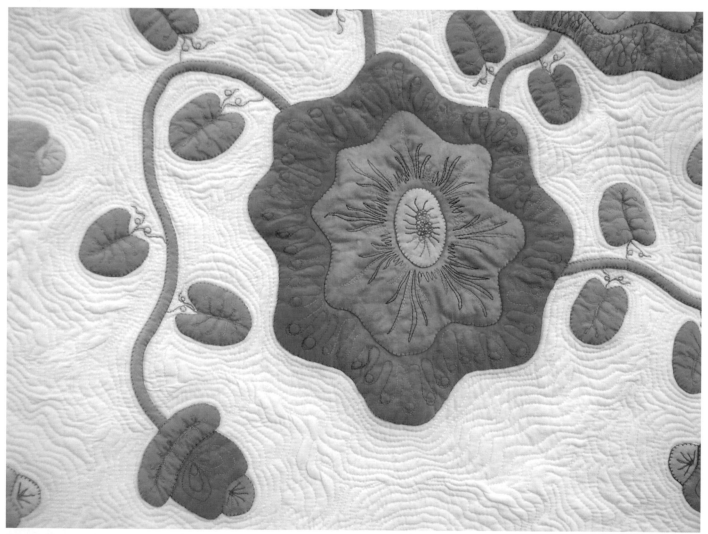

Fig. 2. Trapunto rose

I think of the Rose of Sharon as a "clean and simple" design and I tried not to clutter it up. In the appliqué and in the quilting, I used loose lines and curves and no straight edges. I chose three shades of five different colors of hand-dyed fabrics from a local dyer, Diana Hill. The colors were soft but strong and really "popped" off the white background.

The decorative threadwork was to add interest. I like to create quilts that make an impact from a distance, but also have detail to look at close-up.

Techniques and Essay

I used a freezer-paper technique for my templates. After drawing my design full size on white paper, I traced it backwards onto the dull side of freezer paper with a permanent marker. I ironed the freezer-paper pattern to another layer of freezer paper and cut it out on the lines. This was then ironed to the back side of the material, and cut out by eyeballing a ³⁄₁₆" seam allowance. Clipping was only done when needed to make the piece lie flat. Then starch was sprayed into the lid of the can and applied to the seam allowance with a paintbrush. Using the tip of the iron, I ironed the allowance onto the dull side of the freezer paper. If an area didn't turn out as smooth as I wanted, I just re-starched the area and ironed again. This part took some time, but made it much easier to sew on to the background. I just had to peel the freezer paper off and pin it on (fig. 1).

I used a small buttonhole stitch for the appliqué. I wanted it wide enough to see the variegated thread but not so wide that it would interfere with the trapunto that I added later. A bias bar was used to make the stems.

For the trapunto, I sewed polyester batting to the back of each flower, leaf, and scallop using water-soluble thread. I carefully trimmed the extra batting, layered the quilt with preshrunk cotton batting, and quilted around each motif with invisible thread (figs. 2–3). The "topographic" quilting was done with white rayon thread. I started with one spool of 250 yards and ended up using a little more than four spools. I didn't realize how much more I would need using it on both the top and bobbin (figs. 4–5).

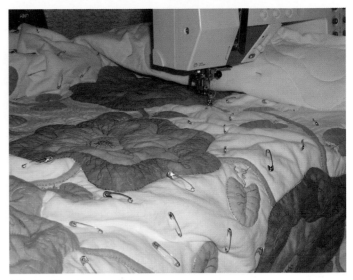

Fig. 3. Trapunto quilting

Fig. 4. Quilting detail

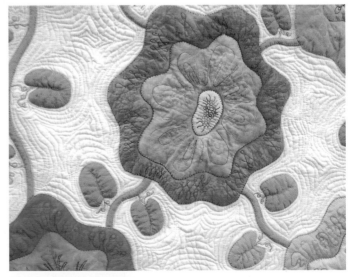

Fig. 5. Quilting detail

Nancy's photo by Mark Hutchison

Finalist
Nancy Hutchison
Kennesaw, Georgia

I have sewn since childhood. My mother, Louise Braman, is an excellent seamstress and she allowed me to play with all her scraps. She also remains my most valued quilt critic. I remember making doll clothes by hand at about age six. My mother taught me to sew on a Singer in a cabinet that used knee control. I think learning how to sew with the knee control has made it very difficult for me to use the knee lift on my Bernina. I seem to revert to my ten-year-old habit of sewing on the Singer, and can't figure out why the machine isn't going!

For my high school graduation I received a portable machine, which allowed me to continue sewing while in college in Kalamazoo. I made extra spending money repairing down jackets in my dorm, as such jackets are required during those long, cold Michigan winters.

I am an active member of the East Cobb Quilt Guild in Marietta, Georgia, and have participated in various workshops from many excellent teachers. I will often sign up for a class that does not particularly interest me because I find that I will always learn something new. My quilt book library and fabric stash are continually growing.

I enjoy sewing with my church group, The Piecemakers. Each of us seeks to donate at least one quilt each year to a person in need or a charitable foundation. My friend Beth Hundt and I enjoy making baby quilts together for coworkers. We shop together when picking the fabrics; Beth pieces the top and I do the quilting. It is a great way to try out new quilting ideas on a smaller scale.

RICK RACK ROSEY
52" x 53"

*It is amazing how many schoolchildren have never seen anybody
hand sew. They are often totally astounded that this is even possible!
One student even asked me, "Isn't there a computer to do that?"*

By profession, I am a registered nurse, working in a fast-paced cardiovascular intensive care unit in Atlanta. I find many nursing skills translate easily to quilting, such as persistence, flexibility, and enjoying the process. Quilting is a meditative activity for me, helping me to dissolve some of the stress accumulated during a typical 12-hour workday. Quilting, just as nursing, can have a strong spiritual component, both involving creating something special for someone else.

Some of the leaves in the sashing were done by hand while I was a camp nurse. In between applying bandages, treating bee stings, and frequent cases of homesickness, I had a few minutes to stitch on the prepared pieces. As always, many questions were aimed at my quilting work such as, "What are you doing?" or, "Why are you doing that?" and once in a while, "Can I try that?" or the dreaded, "How long will that take you to finish?" Students as well as adults were intrigued.

It is amazing how many schoolchildren have never seen anybody hand sew. I did not mention that there are new computerized sewing machines that cost more than my car! Instead, I focused our interaction on the joy of sewing. Hopefully some new appreciation of quilting was fostered.

I have lived in a suburb of Atlanta for the last 18 years with my husband, Mark, a professional photographer, writer, and my own personal art critic, along with our two children, Josiah and Liz. They are puzzled but accepting of my quilting passion. Not to be left out is our beloved dog, Kiah, a four-year old Keeshond, without a doubt the world's smartest dog and my most loyal walking companion. We also share our home with two cats, so I have an unlimited supply of my favorite embellishment, pet hair!

I hope my fascination with fabric will continue to be a creative outlet for me. I feel a strong connection to the quilters of the past and strive to learn from them as much as I do the quilters of today.

Inspiration and Design

I am a member of the Georgia Quilt Council Museum Committee. Our long-term goal is to build a museum in the manner of the Museum of the American Quilter's Society. When I learned that the council planned to pattern four antique quilts that are part of its permanent collection, I was thrilled because one of the quilts is a lovely Rose of Sharon, circa 1875, which I knew would provide inspiration for the New Quilts from Old Favorite contest.

When I have decided on a new quilt design idea, picking fabric is the most exciting part of the creative process for me. The fabric often has a voice of its own. Once the quilt is started, my plans often change and evolve to accommodate the fabric. The excitement of quilting is that I never really know how things will turn out.

Typically, I draw a rough draft of a quilt. I prefer to sew a little, then reevaluate my plan. This is similar to how many painters create their final vision on canvas and makes the creative process very personal.

I updated this classic pattern through color and rickrack embellishment. I used a four-block layout similar to the quilts made in the nineteenth-century era—big blocks with sashing, with the four borders, similar in design yet different.

The four blocks were machine appliquéd with fusible web at the very edges of the shapes and buttonhole-stitched or zigzagged. I get the best results with very fine 50/2 cotton thread matching the color to the appliqué. I stabilized the appliqué with used dryer fabric softener sheets, which you need to trim as they do not tear well. I also starched the background heavily with spray starch right before sewing.

Each large block was made independently of the others. They needed to visually harmonize with each other, and yet still maintain an individual look. I used a lot of freezer-paper drawings to get the proportions just right.

The rickrack was one of those "eureka" moments, occurring while making the third block. I had only a partial package of vintage green cotton rickrack.

Thankfully, my longtime friend and quilting buddy, Jan Cunningham, located more in a box of old supplies. I used every inch!

My original plan for this quilt was for one row of triangles with a wide navy border and fancy quilting. But when I placed extra triangles up on my design wall and noticed how it looked like rickrack, I was thrilled! I really enjoy the rickrack border, and plan to use it again, but next time I will keep a consistent direction. It was difficult to make the second row of triangles cooperate with the direction change. I used the bias square ruler method with bias strip sets to sew the triangles. Although time-consuming, it gave me the best results.

My quilting was delayed for over a week while trying to get my hands on a dark cotton batt but I eventually had to settle for a black poly batt. I enjoy machine quilting and usually plan quilting from the beginning of a new project. The quilting over the roses is created freehand, with a variegated thread. I enjoy the effect of the line disappearing when the thread does not contrast much with the fabric. Echo quilting and background stippling was done with 50-weight cotton thread.

I love the colors in this quilt and the way they interact. I feel the design is a successful adaptation of an old and beautiful pattern using modern colors in a bold manner. My daughter, who has a wonderful way with words, named it RICK RACK ROSEY.

Rickrack and quilting detail

Linda's photo by Julia Johnson

Finalist
Linda Johnson
Monroeville, Indiana

I love every aspect of quilting! I love buying the fabric, creating new designs, piecing, appliquéing, machine quilting, and hanging up the finished piece of art. Quilt shows and competitions rank pretty high, too. My greatest passion is in creating—dreaming up new patterns while non-quilters are sleeping. I learned to sew from my mother when I was in high school. I loved sewing my own clothes, including my wedding dress in 1974. My husband, Gary, and I have a wonderful family of five children and four grandchildren (so far).

In 2001 my sister Jane Wells (this year's fifth place winner!) convinced me to take a quilt class with her and our friend Lynne. That's when I was introduced to my first big quilt show. I was in awe. I had no idea that quilting was such a beautiful, creative, inspiring, and fulfilling art form. I was hooked.

I checked out quilt books by the box load from our library and within weeks, I was designing my own creations. My first design, a Log Cabin variation, was for my daughter's friend Andrea, who was expecting her first child. This quilt was neither square nor flat, but I loved making it and thought it was beautiful.

As I continued taking classes and quilting with my sister, we decided to form our own quilt guild so we would remember to keep time available on our busy calendars to get together for our new passion. We became the Crafty Ol' Broads (she's older, I'm broader). Jane has been my biggest inspiration, always encouraging me and giving me the "you can do it" pep talks. Two years ago we started the Crafty Ol' Broads Pattern Company and teaching

LEAVE ROOM IN YOUR GARDEN FOR FAIRIES TO DANCE

58" x 58"

For me, the best part of teaching is meeting new quilters and watching their love of quilting and creativity grow.

duo, featuring our original quilt patterns. For me, the best part of teaching is meeting new quilters and watching their love of quilting and creativity grow.

In the fall of 2005, during a wonderful vacation in Guatemala, Central America, we fell in love with the beautiful colors and texture of the hand-woven Guatemalan fabric. It was fascinating to watch the native Mayan Indians weave their magic on backstrap looms. We now import the fabric to share through our Crafty Ol' Broads business. Sometimes I design a quilt specifically to showcase the Guatemalan fabric and other times it just seems to coordinate beautifully with my rather large stash of domestic fabrics.

Quilting has become very important to me and I am lucky that my husband and children have been so supportive. Our family and extended family is very close, and nothing could ever be more important than they are. I hope to inspire an appreciation of this wonderful art in them, and I love gifting them with my quilts that will someday be passed on to their children. My dreams of the future include writing quilt books and teaching on a larger scale. I already have several book themes in mind and sometimes think of my latest creation, "Wouldn't this be a great book cover?"

Inspiration and Design

I am often inspired by antique quilts. Floral appliqué quilts are especially interesting to me. I saw a garden sign in a shop that said, "Leave room in your garden for the fairies to dance" and immediately knew that it would be the name of a future quilt. When I saw the announcement for this contest, I started doodling flower blocks and dancing fairies.

The background fabrics are the wonderfully textured Guatemalan handwoven cottons. I pieced the colorful stripes in a square-in-a-square design with value changes for depth and luminosity. This created the challenge of appliquéing on a completed quilt top rather than on separate blocks, but the end result was worth the extra effort. All of the appliqués are bright, light domestic cottons to contrast with the darker background. I wanted fairy wings so delicate

you could see through them, so I chose organza with built-in sparkle.

My original draft had nine different flower designs with identical vine shapes meeting to form a crisscross grid across the quilt but when I was placing the appliqués on the design wall, they looked too cluttered. I designed alternate blocks of different shapes and left blank spaces between the flowers to give the eyes a place to rest and allow the background stripes to show through the appliqués. The sunflowers got the space of two blocks because of their size and I love the asymmetrical look it gives to the completed quilt.

I patterned the fairy in the lower right corner from a photograph of a friend's daughter, Eve, when she was a young ballerina. That set the stage for the size and shape of the rest of the fairies. As I fine-tuned my drawings, I decided the fairies needed music to dance to, so I added a whimsical frog playing his drum. His stage is a three-dimensional sunflower leaf. The praying mantis is just there to enjoy the show.

I chose to do raw-edge appliqué with machine blanket stitch, a technique I learned in a great Sue Nickels' class. I fused all the appliqués on the entire quilt first because I wanted the freedom to change my mind on placement and colors before I started any blanket stitching. After auditioning several decorative quilting threads, I finally chose invisible nylon thread to do my free-motion machine quilting because the other colors interfered with the striped fabric.

The border fabric continues the luminosity within the quilt. For the side borders, I pieced quarter-square triangles with the Guatemalan fabric, matching the stripes within each square. All of the piecing, appliquéing, and quilting were done on my home sewing machine, and it took seven months to complete. It's been a true labor of love and my most challenging quilt to date.

Piecing the Striped Background

After sketching the initial quilt design, I drew the square-in-a-square background on graph paper to determine the finished measurements of each segment of the design (fig. 1). The background is made up of four squares in four different fabrics, and each square has four mitered corners. You can use this technique for any size quilt top using the following steps:

1. Using your measurements from your graph paper, draw each triangle and trapezoid piece in one-quarter of the quilt, full-size, onto freezer paper. Cut the pattern pieces out.

2. Reassemble and pin these freezer-paper patterns onto your design wall to ensure that each mitered edge will meet correctly with its adjoining piece, leaving no gaps. Label each pattern piece with its intended location and fabric name.

3. Press the freezer-paper patterns onto the wrong side of your fabric.

   If you're using striped fabric, special care must be taken to match the stripes at all 16 mitered seams. Place the outside edge of each pattern piece in one fabric group on the same stripe, or identical repeat of that stripe.

4. Cut fabric, adding a ¼" seam allowance. Repeat for all four different fabrics in all four sections of the quilt.

5. You will now be working with many bias edges, so be careful. Sew each center light purple triangle to its adjoining dark purple trapezoid to form four center quarter-square triangles.

6. Join the four quarter-square triangles to form the center square.

7. Sew each light blue triangle to its adjoining dark blue trapezoid. Join two of these units to form the quilt top's corner triangles. Make four.

8. Sew one corner triangle to each side of the center square.

The background is now ready for the appliqués.

Fusible, Raw-edge Appliqués with Blanket Stitch

The poses for the fairies were inspired by pictures of dancers, skaters, and gymnasts. I simplified my drawings to accommodate the appliqué process. Because I was appliquéing onto a dark background,

I fused two pieces of skin fabric together to prevent the dark background from showing through. All the pieces of one flower or fairy were fused together before placing them on the background.

I drew my master designs onto tracing paper. When I arranged the appliqués onto the background, I checked for placement accuracy by placing the tracing paper master over the appliqués before fusing them. I used a variety of thread types and colors for the blanket stitching, sometimes matching the appliqué and other times adding detail with a coordinating color. I used metallic silver to blanket-stitch the fairy wings.

I would like to expand this quilt design into a pattern to sell and teach. I will redesign it so that each flower section is on its own separate block. That would make the blanket-stitch technique much easier to handle. You could make a smaller wall-hanging of your favorite blocks or increase the size to a bed quilt. It could also be designed for different seasons. Oh, the endless possibilities—I think I feel another sleepless night ahead of me.

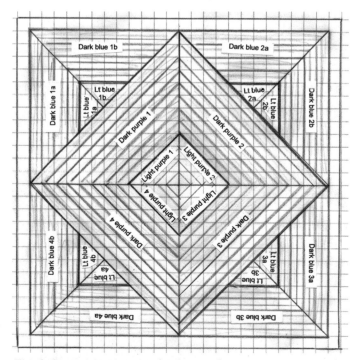

Fig. 1. Square-in-a-square background

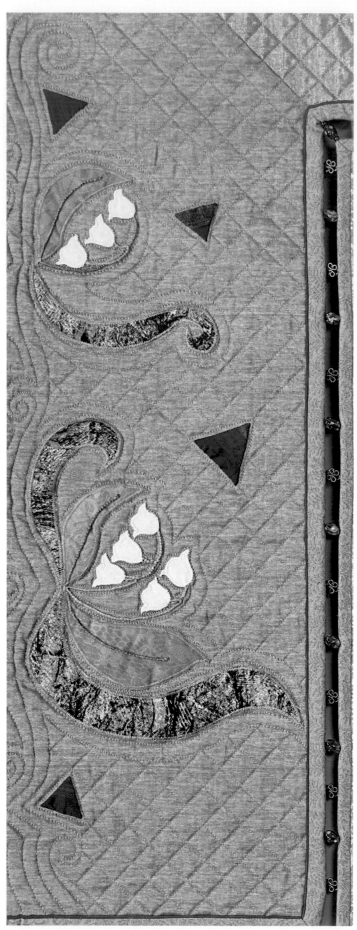

How-to photos by Chris Lynn Kirsch

Finalist
Chris Lynn Kirsch
Watertown, Wisconsin
& Sharon Rotz
Mosinee, Wisconsin

Meet Chris (on the right)
I began quilting in 1987 when my sister-in-law talked me into taking a class. By 1992 I was teaching at a local technical college and with time and the guidance of excellent teachers, I began to leave patterns behind and create my own work. My quilting evolution has left me with a passion for antique, traditional, contemporary, and art quilts. I love it all.

The idea for collaborating on our first quilt came about when two different topics of conversation morphed into one big challenge. I had shared with Sharon details of an Anything Goes challenge originated by the Milwaukee Art Quilters. She was hooked on the idea. Then she and I discussed how we were both intrigued by the New Quilts from an Old Favorite contest. Thus our first quilt collaboration was born. We have been encouraged to continue the partnership and we are very pleased that our hybrid rose is a success.

I enjoy how working with Sharon causes me to stretch outside of my comfort zone and strive to do my best work. I also love to create my own work and share my passion with others. Besides teaching, creating, and writing, my quilting led me and another dear friend, Wendy Rieves, into a partnership with a travel agent and together we organize and lead quilting cruises throughout the world.

ROSE OF CHRIS AND SHARON
63" x 63"

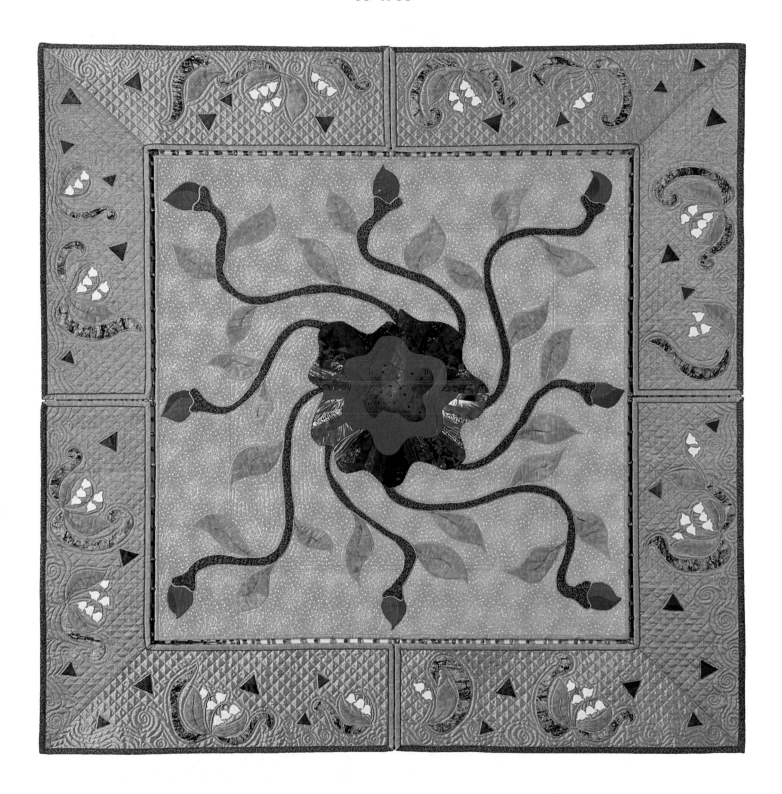

Working long distance and cooperating on a quilt brings struggles, but by exploring new solutions and combining our talents we feel richly rewarded.

Rose of Sharon: New Quilts from an Old Favorite

69

Meet Sharon (on the left)

I met Chris several years ago at a quilting retreat where we were both teaching. We immediately felt a close bond and have been friends ever since. This is our third quilt together, and each quilt has been an adventure and a positive learning experience. Our previous quilt was conceived and started on a weekend together. This quilt was done with a round robin approach, with the quilt constantly being shipped back and forth. I think I prefer the former approach because of the immediate feedback from bouncing ideas back and forth. Had Chris been at my side, I'm sure she would have pointed out the folly of completely machine piecing the center rose. Both approaches to working together have their own merits and have challenged us in different ways.

Since we are both authors and teachers of our own techniques, it is definitely stimulating to try to merge our ideas and work as a team. I have been teaching quiltmaking for twenty years and love sharing ideas and techniques with other quilters. I enjoy making art quilts, which have hung in many art gallery exhibits. As a textile artist, I have been commissioned by medical facilities, museums, and numerous private collectors.

I love color and am constantly trying new or unusual combinations. While realism has definite merit, it is personally more rewarding to abstract images and work with the abundance of fabric options available. I'm constantly exploring and branching out in new directions. I feel there is so much left to do and quilting will be a part of my life for many more years.

The Collaboration

Chris and Sharon live 150 miles apart so this project came together via the U.S. Postal Service and lots of e-mails. One would make a start, mail it to the other, then she would do whatever she felt was needed, and mail it back. This continued until the quilt was completed.

Sharon got the ball rolling by free-form piecing four large roses. Chris decided to use just one and added octopus stems and buds. She used her repliqué technique to make the buds. Sharon worked her free-motion quilting magic, designed the lily of the valley patterns for the border, and returned the quilted center section along with the cotton lamé border fabric.

Chris repliquéd the flowers and leaves in the border strips. Sharon assembled and quilted the border strips and Chris finished them with piped binding and a total of 24 mitered corners! The five sections were joined with a beading technique Chris calls "crossings," in which "the beads cross the gap and hold the broken pieces of my quilt together as my faith in the cross of Christ holds the broken pieces of my life together."

Design and Inspiration:
Sharon

Just as the quilters of times past related their quilt blocks to their lives, we continue in that tradition. We started with the Bible verse for which the Rose of Sharon pattern is named. We chose wild roadside roses and the lily of the valley to tell its tale.

Lilies of the valley have always been a part of my mother's garden and my own, and I have always associated them with the Bible verse. This hardy and unassuming garden plant bursts out with showy bells and overwhelming fragrance just as the roadside rose enchants us with its fragrance and wild beauty.

In this quilt, we chose the rose as the dominant feature but we wanted some elements of the quilt to be hidden from first view. We attempted to create depth in the design to entice the viewer to come in closer. I quilted the lilies into the background of the rose, their beauty hidden at first glance, just as the beauty of the beloved might have been overlooked. Only those who take the time to study this work will enjoy the detail of the quilting, appliqué, and the beaded borders.

Creating Original Quilting Designs:
Sharon

The first step in making original quilting designs is to determine the size needed. This is often dictated by the size of the border or quilt block. If not, select a size proportional to your quilt size. For border designs, divide the length into segments. Design your quilting elements to fit into these spaces.

Because I was going to machine quilt this project, I wanted continuous-line designs to avoid a lot of starting and stopping. I wanted the design to fill the area and include curving and curling lines, which I find easier to quilt than straight lines. After drawing several choices, combining, refining, and working with them, I finally arrived at my quilting choices (see fig. 7, page 73).

I transferred the design to tracing paper and made several copies that were pinned in place on the quilt. I quilted through the tracing paper and removed it after the quilting. Although this is a tedious task, I prefer it to trying to remove markings from my quilt top. The tracing-paper patterns are easy to see and therefore faster to quilt and I don't have to make all my quilting decisions before I baste my quilt.

Repliqué Technique:
Chris

I have been using my repliqué technique to re-create pictures and drawings in machine appliqué since the early 1990s. I love the accurate results that can be achieved without fusibles, templates, or a degree in art!

1. Copy the rosebud pattern onto plain copier paper. The finished block will be a reverse of the pattern (fig. 1).

2. Determine the order of appliqué by starting with whatever is farthest back and working forward. The sequence for this pattern is:
    (1) background, (2) light petal,
    (3) dark petal, and (4) stem.

3. Cut a piece of the background fabric large enough to cover the pattern and lay it on the work surface wrong-side up. Place the pattern right-side up on top of the background fabric and pin it in place at the four corners.

4. Cut a piece of the lighter petal fabric a little larger than the area it will cover on the pattern and place the wrong side of it against the right side of the background fabric. Hold everything up to the light, looking from the pattern side, to ensure that the petal fabric is over the area it will cover. Secure it with transparent tape (fig. 2).

5. Thread the machine with a color to match the lighter petal fabric in both the top and the bobbin.

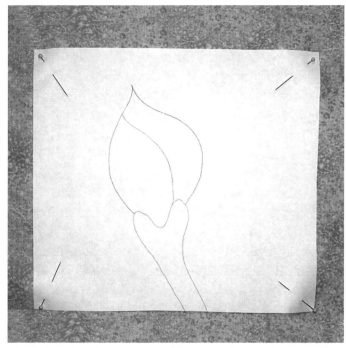

Fig. 1. Rosebud in reverse

Fig. 2. Petal fabric secured with tape

Fig. 3. Stitching the petal

Fig. 4. Trimming the petal

Fig. 5. Satin stitching the petal

6. Working from the pattern side, free-motion straight stitch on the lines of the lighter petal (fig. 3).

7. Turn to the fabric side. With a sharp scissors, trim away the excess light petal fabric very close to the stitching (fig. 4).

8. Satin stitch along the edge that will not be covered by the darker petal fabric (fig. 5). Be sure the satin stitch is wide enough to cover both the bobbin thread from the previous straight stitching and the raw edge.

9. Repliqué the darker petal in the same manner, satin stitching all edges that will not be covered by the stem.

10. Repliqué the stem. The bud is complete (fig. 6).

11. Remove the paper.

Fig. 6. Finished rosebud

Fig. 7. Lily-of-the-Valley quilting designs

Finalist

Yoshiko Kobayashi

Katano City, Osaka, Japan

In the late 1980s I started making quilts, inspired by a quilt exhibition. Like almost all beginning quilters in Japan, I made bags, cushions, small tapestries, and other items. But I wanted to be able to make big quilting projects some day.

Until attending a workshop with Nancy Crow in Osaka, Japan, all my quilts were hand pieced and hand quilted. Since then, I have also been influenced by lessons from Melody Johnson and Libby Lehman.

For me, as a self-taught quilter, the invitation to enter a contest gives me a chance for more quiltmaking and inspiration. I especially like designing under the kind of restrictions of the New Quilts from an Old Favorite contest.

When my quilt, JOY OF GARDENER, won first place in the Seven Sisters contest in 2005, my husband and I made our first trip to Paducah and visited the quilt museum. Going to the AQS Quilt Show & Contest had been my dearest wish. It was very exciting for me.

I would like to make more quilts in the future with something natural and close to me, such as flowers, trees, or landscapes.

Inspiration and Design

I love roses but I'm not so good at making them grow. I think they're delicate, or maybe insects make them ill. Or it may be that my mind is too

RAMBLER ROSE

70" x 72"

I wanted to express my image of a rambler rose hedge in full bloom on my quilt.

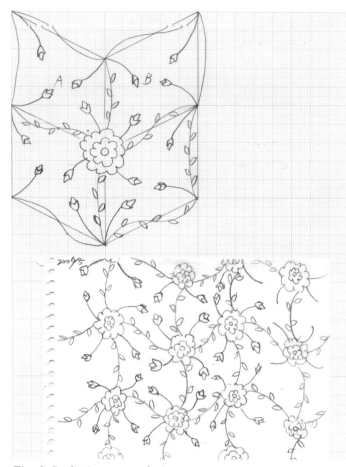

Fig. 1. Preliminary rose design

much on my quilting. I dream of having our hedge with lots of flowers of rambler roses. I wanted to express my image of a rambler rose hedge in full bloom on my quilt.

On my diagram of the repeating pattern, I challenged myself to express the nice deep coloration, the beautiful curved line of the vine, and the loveliness of the flowers with a complicated surface design.

First, I tried to do a sketch on paper of the images I wanted to make (figs. 1–2). Then I made a background plan (fig. 3). After making some copies of the background plan, I colored it in with pencils (fig. 4). Then I pieced the background according to my plan and applied the border. I wanted the background to have nice depth.

I tried different colors for the vines and appliquéd the vines and stems onto the background (fig. 5). I appliquéd large leaves on the vines and smaller leaves on the stems.

I cut out the flower shapes. The large flower centers were made by stamping a lace pattern on white fabric

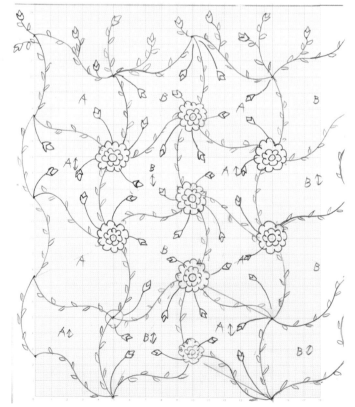

Fig. 2. Preliminary rose design

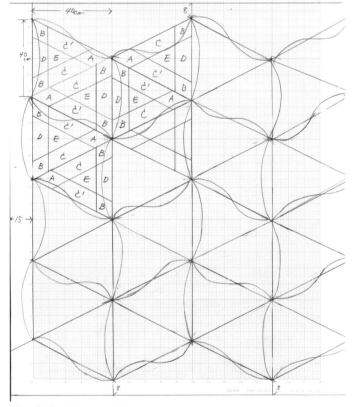

Fig. 3. Background design

and then cutting out the shapes. The centers were sewn to the flowers with a machine zigzag stitch, then trimmed from the back with a .5 cm seam allowance.

I appliquéd green circles by machine in the center of medium-sized flowers and trimmed them from the back with a .5 cm seam allowance. I cut them in quarters for the large rosebuds and in eighths for the small rosebuds (fig. 6). I arranged the dark-colored flowers and rosebuds on the lower part of the quilt and the light colors on the upper part.

The work of filling up all the large space with appliqué after making the whole background distressed me. I had to do the appliqué work while turning the large pieced background fabric in all directions. It was hard work and took many days during the hot summer. I thought that this project might have been a terrible plan.

But after continuing the work every day, the surface of the quilt was filled. I was so happy putting the last flower onto my quilt.

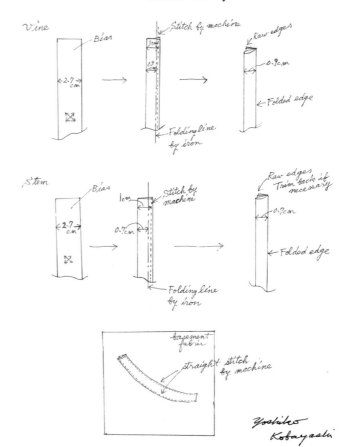

Fig. 5. Stem and vine construction plan

Fig. 4. Rose and background design

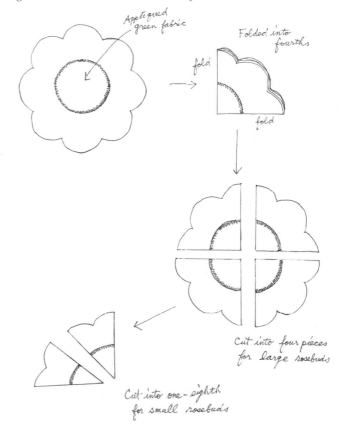

Fig. 6. Rosebud construction plan

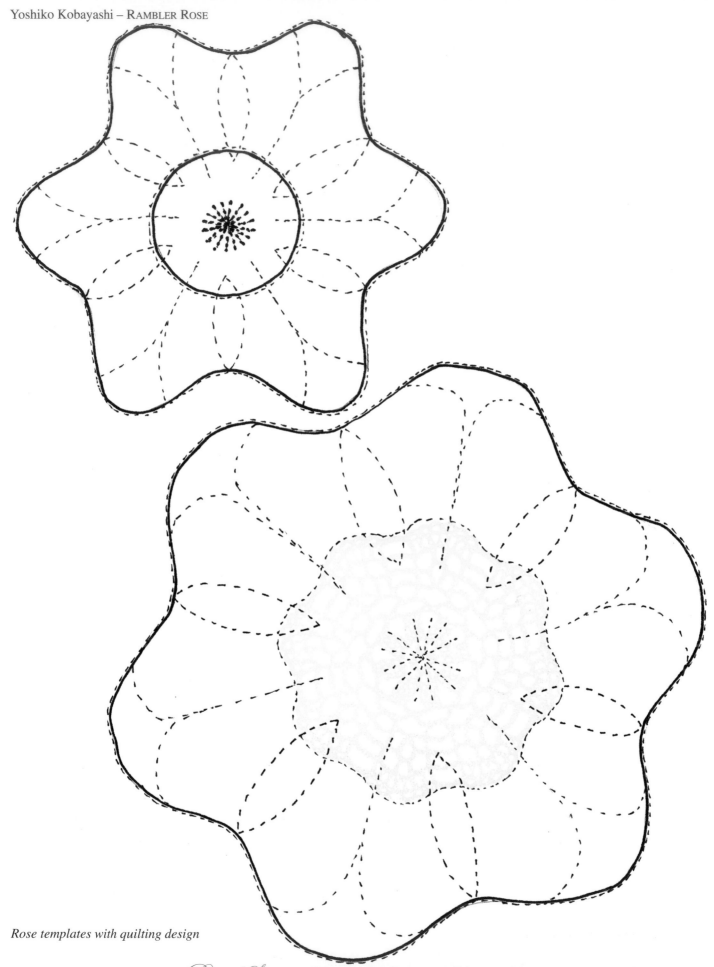

Rose templates with quilting design

Rose of Sharon: New Quilts from an Old Favorite

Rose templates with quilting design

Nancy Lambert

Pittsburgh, Pennsylvania

I have sewed clothing and accessories from a very young age. I became interested in quilting more than twenty years ago as an extension of my sewing hobby. I have since quit sewing clothes and have concentrated on making quilts.

I am especially interested in creating new designs and design techniques. I have used a graded fabric technique in this quilt and included the use of machine-embroidery techniques that complement the fabric designs. I like to explore and extend the possibilities of the technology that machine embroidery provides along with the traditional aspects of quilting.

Trying to find time to fit quilting into the daily business of life is always a challenge. I will sketch out a particular design while waiting to pick up a child from a sports event or in any few minutes in between activities. I have a room set up with the sewing machines, ironing board, and other necessities so that it is easily accessible for even a few minutes of quilting.

Inspiration and Design

I have always been interested in flowers and like incorporating them into quilts, either by use of the colors within a flower or with the actual flower itself. Many of the choices I make for a quilt's colors are often based upon colors seen in nature. I have made interpretations of flowers in the past such as hydrangeas, sunflowers, and pansies. I wanted to make a rose and try some new ideas I had.

First I tried piecing fabric I'd dyed, then I tried fabric I'd painted. The results both times had a nice look to them, but I wanted the texture that

ROSE OF SAMANTHA
58½" x 63"

I like to explore and extend the possibilities of the technology that machine embroidery provides along with the traditional aspects of quilting.

Fig. 1. Graded embroidered rose

Fig. 2. Grading enhanced by pinking the edges

patterned fabric adds. I chose to use multiple calico prints and cut them up and grade them to achieve shaded results.

I was pleased with the large rose and the gradual shading that was achieved by grading the fabrics. From a distance the individual rose petals appear to be of one fabric. I believe that the variety of fabrics used for each petal and leaf added a dimensional quality to the rose.

Techniques

I created a line drawing of the rose and drew the individual petals, breaking up each petal into smaller shapes. For the large rose petals, I chose four to six calico prints and positioned them based on value. I used large zigzag cuts to soften and blend the edges (see photo on page 80). I fused the layers of each petal and appliquéd the finished petals in place.

For the smaller roses and rosebuds around the border, I digitized the image into my computer and created an embroidery design that I stitched out on my Bernina machine (fig. 1). Each embroidered rose was done in six to eight different threads. The shades of thread were chosen to replicate the light and dark of the petals. The embroidered roses also incorporated a smaller zigzag edge between each color transition.

Templates are provided for you to try the grading technique on a simple flower shape.

The flower can be graded from a light outer ring to a dark center or from a dark outer ring to a light center. The additional layers of fabric help blend the color. The blending can be enhanced by softening the edges with pinking shears (fig. 2).

Template for making graded rose

Finalist

Bev Munson & Sandie Dolbee

Kalamazoo, Michigan

Meet Beverly

In 1975, after years of garment sewing, I started a crib quilt while pregnant with our "bicentennial baby." The gingham dog and calico cat design came from a McCall's publication and seemed simple enough. A friend taught me the basics of hand appliqué and I was on my way. I finished it just in time for my son's first birthday.

Since that time quilting has been an energizing force in my life—the ideas, designs, colors, and fabrics, the process of sewing by hand or machine, and especially the times with quilting friends. I am a cofounder of our local guild, the Kalamazoo Log Cabin Quilters, which recently celebrated its 25th anniversary. It is a wonderful resource for the community.

I enjoy all aspects of quilting and have tried to learn a variety of techniques. That way, I have a wide vocabulary of skills I can call on, enabling me to solve problems creatively. My favorite part is choosing the colors and fabrics. Most of my quilts use hundreds of fabrics in a controlled, scrappy manner.

I find that quilting provides endless opportunities for learning and creativity, and great satisfaction in seeing ideas take shape as each step is completed. Being challenged to try a different technique, a more complex pattern, a new material or tool, builds on everything I've done before. To communicate a feeling, share an image, or

Beverly's photo by James W. Munson; Sandie's photo by Frank Severance

CRACKLIN' ROSIE

55½" x 55½"

*We chose to use a scrappy background in part because
it would take advantage of our strengths as quilters.*

reinterpret a traditional pattern is very satisfying. I also enjoy collaborating to create quilts for a raffle, a charity, or a competition. It is lots of fun to work together and the results reflect that.

The support of my family and friends pushes me to continually grow as a quilter, to use the ideas I've gathered, and to apply techniques and skills I've learned. I love to travel and attend quilt shows, take workshops and lectures, and to find ideas wherever they may wait.

Meet Sandie

My interest in quilting started in the early 1970s. At that time there were relatively few books, no rotary cutters or mats, and cotton fabric was mostly calicos and hard to come by where I lived. I didn't know anyone else who made quilts except my mother who lived two hours away. She made doll bed quilts for my daughter, all by hand. So I read what I could, used what she showed me, and started in.

I used cereal boxes for cardboard templates, traced each piece on the fabric, cut them out with scissors

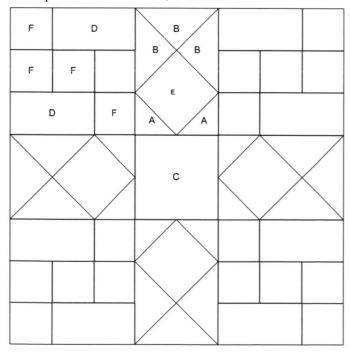

Fig. 1. Michigan Arrowhead block

and stitched them together by hand. Thankfully we now have an abundance of tools to speed up the process! Fabric was purchased for each specific project and I didn't know about stashes, even though I saved all the scraps, just like I did with the leftovers from making clothes.

Eventually I discovered *Quilter's Newsletter Magazine* (still in black-and-white) and fellow quilters. Friends of my parents gave me quilts and quilt tops that had been stored away for years and I got a few quilts and boxes of blocks at auctions. I was hooked. As cotton fabrics became more available, I become more interested in scrap quilts. As one of my friends says, "All reds go together if you use enough different ones."

Since that time my interest has evolved into a passion for drafting and designing complex pieced quilts and for precision piecing. I have developed workshops that emphasize the drafting as well as the piecing of Eight-Pointed Star and Mariner's Compass blocks.

My husband also enjoys attending shows with me. We admire the accomplishments of the talented quilters and I always get ideas that I just can't wait to try.

Bev and I met in a class in Houston. We met again when my husband and I moved to Kalamazoo. In many ways we are alike: we are willing to try new ideas and methods, we both like gardening, especially daylilies, and cooking, especially soups and breads. But we are also different: I have two dogs (Matilda and Samantha), she has two cats (Cosie and Violet); she lives on a lake, I live in the woods; she loves appliqué, I like intricate piecing; she goes first for color and fabric, I go more towards drafting and design. But we both like to share, help others, and bounce ideas off each other.

Quilt Construction

We chose to use a scrappy background. The Michigan Arrowhead block had a good variety of shapes and sizes, allowing us to set certain rules for how we laid out the color (fig.1). The tiny triangles at the interior of each star could act as sparklers if we assigned them a light value, creating small-scaled points of interest. The diagonally-set squares helped encourage a sense of movement. We gave them a medium value to play off of the light-hued triangles and help generate a rhythmic flow across the entire background. For the star points, we chose one fabric to help the viewer read the star as a cohesive shape. Finally, we selected interesting and complex fabrics for the large squares so that the viewer could enjoy the printed texture of the fabric.

We started by pulling 100+ light-valued fabrics that we had in blues, blue-greens, and lavenders to create a constant value with a variety of textures. Then we worked through the fabrics in the first round of edits, sorting the already light-valued fabrics into light, medium, and dark piles.

To begin building the background, we rotary cut the different shapes of the pattern in the fabrics that we thought would work best (fig. 2). We laid out the entire background on a flannel-covered wall, continuously editing according to the loose rules we had set for which value went where. If any fabric still read as a pattern at a distance of six feet, we put it into the reject pile.

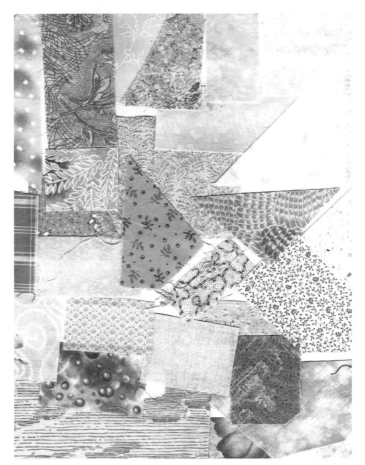

Fig. 2. Background pieces

After we were satisfied with the background, we split the quilt in two so that each of us could work on piecing. When the blocks were completely pieced, we set them together in four quadrants to make the appliqué process simpler.

The appliqué work was done in the four sections until the very end, when the quadrants were joined and the other half of the stems could be appliquéd to the next quadrant. Finally, the large central motif was added. We primarily used the needle-turn technique with starch and freezer paper as needed (fig. 3).

The only fabrics we purchased specifically for the project were the backing and the border. The green border turned out to be different from the hot pink batik we had originally planned, as so often happens. We did find a home for that batik as it worked perfectly as the piping accent. We used plastic overlays to plan the quilting design, which was completed by Pam Huggins of Kalamazoo, Michigan.

Fig. 3. Positioning the appliqué

How-to photos by Beverly Munson

8" block

12" block

12" block

12" block

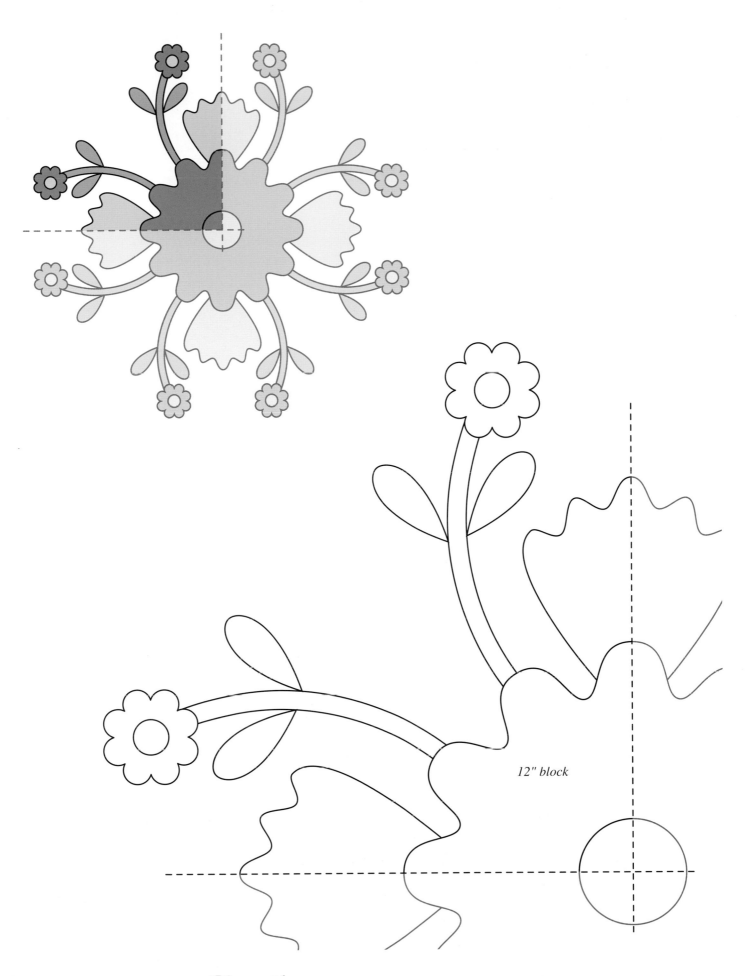

12" block

12" block

Books

Brackman, Barbara. *Encyclopedia of Appliqué: An Illustrated, Numerical Index to Traditional and Modern Patterns.* McLean, VA: EPM Publications, Inc., 1993.

Critchlow, Keith. *Islamic Patterns, an Analytical and Cosmological Approach.* Rochester, VT: Inner Traditions, 1999.

Hall, Jane and Dixie Haywood. *Foundation Quilts: Building on the Past.* Paducah, KY: American Quilter's Society, 2000.

Havig, Bettina. *Carrie Hall Blocks: Over 800 Historical Patterns from the College of the Spencer Museum of Art, University of Kansas.* Paducah, KY: American Quilter's Society, 1999.

Kirsch, Chris Lynn. *Repliqué Quilts: Appliqué Designs from Favorite Photos.* Woodinville, WA: Martingale Publishing, 2001.

Mathieson, Judy. *Mariner's Compass Quilts: New Directions.* Lafayette, CA: C&T Publishing, 1995.

Robinson, Jodi. *Creative Alternatives for Traditional Favorites.* Vancouver, WA: Columbia River Quilting & Design, 2004.

Rotz, Sharon V. *Log Cabin Quilts with Attitude.* Iola, WI: Krause Publications, 2006.

Safford, Carleton L. and Robert Bishop. *America's Quilts and Coverlets.* New York, NY: Weathervane Books, 1974.

Web Sites

Chris Lynn Kirsch: www.chrisquilts.net

Jane K. Wells and Linda Johnson: www.craftyolbroads.com

Karen Kay Buckley Perfect Circles™ templates: www.karenkaybuckley.com

Natural Intelligence Custom Fibonacci Spiral Generator: http://chromatism.net/cfsg.htm

Mary Vaneecke: www.elsolquilting.com

Sharon V. Rotz: www.bysher.net

The Museum of the

MAQS is the world's largest and foremost museum devoted to quilts and the only museum dedicated to today's quilts and quiltmakers. Established in 1991 by AQS founders Bill and Meredith Schroeder as a not-for-profit organization, MAQS is located in a 27,000 square-foot facility. It was designed specifically to display quilts effectively and safely. Three expansive galleries envelop visitors in color, exquisite stitchery, and design.

The highlight of any visit is The William & Meredith Schroeder Gallery, which exhibits a rotating installation of quilts from the museum's permanent collection of over 250 quilts. Before MAQS opened, the Schroeders had acquired a private collection of remarkable quilts. In addition to being a source of wonder for the collectors, the collection came to recognize extraordinary contemporary quilts and their makers. Through the Schroeders' generosity, the nucleus of the museum collection was formed. In addition, the permanent collection includes award-winning quilts from the annual AQS Quilt Show & Contest. In 2006, MAQS added "Oh, Wow!" a stunning collection of more than 40 miniature quilts to the permanent collection. Educational programs

offered in three well-equipped classrooms serve local and national audiences. Specifically, MAQS offers an annual schedule of in-depth workshops taught by master quilters. Children and families can participate in hands-on projects. Exhibitions developed by MAQS, like New Quilts from an Old Favorite, travel to other galleries and museums, helping educate and inspire a wider spectrum of viewers. With more than 1000 quilt-related book titles available, the museum's bookstore has one of the largest selections of quilt books anywhere. In addition, the bookstore offers special quilt-related merchandise as well as fine crafts by artisans

Photos by Jessica Byassee

American Quilter's Society (MAQS)

from this region and beyond. The entire facility is wheelchair accessible.

Located at 215 Jefferson Street in historic downtown Paducah, Kentucky, MAQS is open year-round 10A.M. to 5 P.M., Monday through Saturday. From April 1 through October 31, it is also open Sundays from 1 to 5 P.M. For extended hours during special events such as the AQS Quilt Show, Second Saturdays in conjunction with the LowerTown Arts District, and others, please check the MAQS Web site listed below.

The museum programs can also be sampled on the Web site: www.quiltmuseum.org.
For more information,
e-mail: info@quiltmuseum.org
call: (270) 442-8856
or write: MAQS
PO Box 1540
Paducah, KY 42002-1540

Other AQS Books

This is only a small selection of the books available from the American Quilter's Society. AQS books are known worldwide for timely topics, clear writing, beautiful color photos, and accurate illustrations and patterns. The following books are available from your local bookseller, quilt shop, or public library.

#7018   *us$24.95*

#6905   *us$24.95*

#6804   *us$22.95*

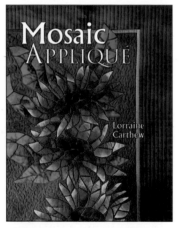

#7071   *us$22.95*

#7086 *8" x 8"*   *us$24.95*

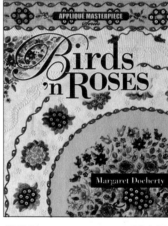

#7013   *us$24.95*

#7073   *us$24.95*

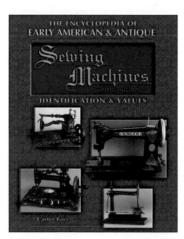

#7042 (HB)   *us$29.95*

#6899   *us$21.95*

LOOK for these books nationally.
CALL or **VISIT** our Web site at

1-800-626-5420
www.AmericanQuilter.com